THE
100+
SERIES™

Reproducible Activities

Intro to Geometry

Grades 5–8

by
Mary Lee Vivian
Tammy Bohn-Voepel
Margaret Thomas

Instructional Fair
An imprint of Carson-Dellosa Publishing LLC
Greensboro, North Carolina

Instructional Fair

Authors: Mary Lee Vivian, Tammy Bohn-Voepel, Margaret Thomas
Editor: Jerry Aten

Instructional Fair
An imprint of Carson-Dellosa Publishing LLC
PO Box 35665
Greensboro, NC 27425 USA

ISBN 978-0-74241-777-9
01-182117784

NCTM Standards of Math for Grades 6-8

Note to Teacher: Each activity in this book has been linked to the related NCTM Standards listed below. The numbers of the related Standards for each activity are indicated in the Table of Contents.

1. Number and Operations – Understand numbers, ways of representing numbers, relationships among numbers, and number systems. Understand meanings of operations and how they relate to one another. Compute fluently and make reasonable estimates.

2. Algebra – Understand patterns, relations, and functions. Represent and analyze mathematical situations and structures using algebraic symbols. Use mathematical models to represent and understand quantitative relationships. Analyze change in various contexts.

3. Geometry – Analyze characteristics and properties of two- and three-dimensional geometric shapes and develop mathematical arguments about geometric relationships. Specify locations and describe spatial relationships using coordinate geometry and other representational systems. Apply transformations and use symmetry to analyze mathematical situations. Use visualization, spatial reasoning, and geometric modeling to solve problems.

4. Measurement – Understand measurable attributes of objects and the units, systems, and processes of measurement. Apply appropriate techniques, tools, and formulas to determine measurements.

5. Data Analysis and Probability – Formulate questions that can be addressed with data and collect, organize, and display relevant data to answer them. Select and use appropriate statistical methods to analyze data. Develop and evaluate inferences and predictions that are based on data. Understand and apply basic concepts of probability.

6. Problem Solving – Build new mathematical knowledge through problem solving. Solve problems that arise in mathematics and in other contexts. Apply and adapt a variety of appropriate strategies to solve problems. Monitor and reflect on the process of mathematical problem solving.

7. Reasoning and Proof – Recognize reasoning and proof as fundamental aspects of mathematics. Make and investigate mathematical conjectures. Develop and evaluate mathematical arguments and proofs. Select and use various types of reasoning and methods of proof.

8. Communication – Organize and consolidate their mathematical thinking through communication. Communicate their mathematical thinking coherently and clearly to peers, teachers, and others. Analyze and evaluate the mathematical thinking and strategies of others. Use the language of mathematics to express mathematical ideas precisely.

9. Connections – Recognize and use connections among mathematical ideas. Understand how mathematical ideas interconnect and build on one another to produce a coherent whole. Recognize and apply mathematics in contexts outside of mathematics.

10. Representation – Create and use representations to organize, record, and communicate mathematical ideas. Select, apply, and translate among mathematical representations to solve problems. Use representations to model and interpret physical, social, and mathematical phenomena.

Table of Contents

Table of Contents Continued

Name _____   Date _____

Congruence and Addition Properties of Segments

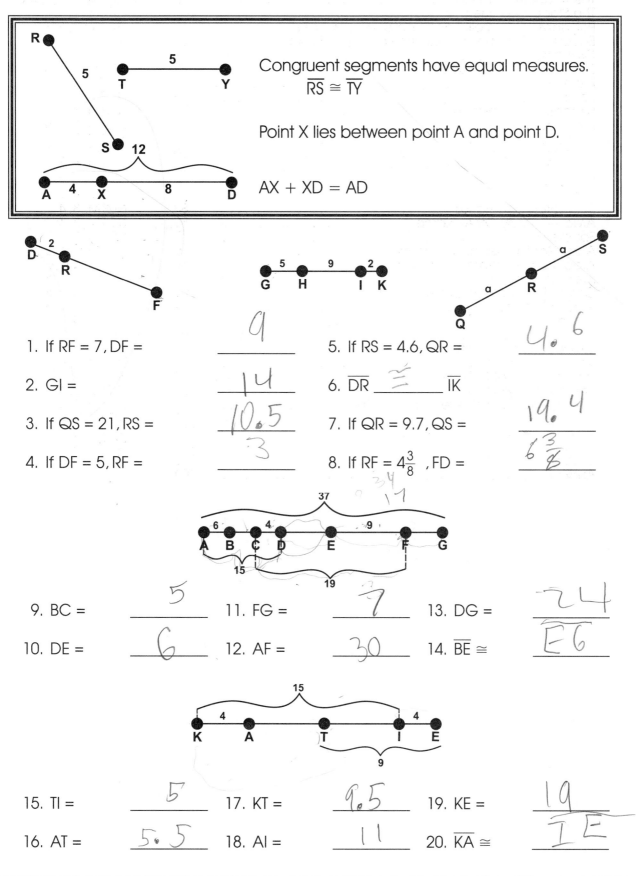

Congruent segments have equal measures.
$\overline{RS} \cong \overline{TY}$

Point X lies between point A and point D.

$AX + XD = AD$

1. If RF = 7, DF = _____ 9

2. GI = _____ 14

3. If QS = 21, RS = _____ 10.5

4. If DF = 5, RF = _____ 3

5. If RS = 4.6, QR = _____ 4.6

6. $\overline{DR}$ ___$\cong$___ $\overline{IK}$

7. If QR = 9.7, QS = _____ 19.4

8. If RF = $4\frac{3}{8}$, FD = _____ $6\frac{3}{8}$

9. BC = _____ 5

10. DE = _____ 6

11. FG = _____ 7

12. AF = _____ 30

13. DG = _____ 24

14. $\overline{BE} \cong$ _____ $\overline{EG}$

15. TI = _____ 5

16. AT = _____ 5.5

17. KT = _____ 9.5

18. AI = _____ 11

19. KE = _____ 19

20. $\overline{KA} \cong$ _____ $\overline{IE}$

Name _____   Date _____

Angles

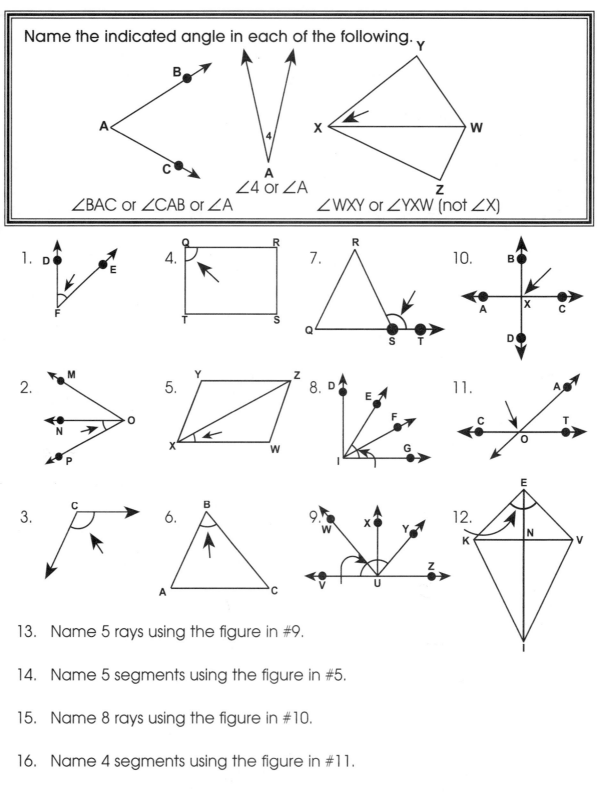

Name the indicated angle in each of the following.

∠BAC or ∠CAB or ∠A   ∠4 or ∠A   ∠WXY or ∠YXW (not ∠X)

1.

4.

7.

10.

2.

5.

8.

11.

3.

6.

9.

12.

13.   Name 5 rays using the figure in #9.

14.   Name 5 segments using the figure in #5.

15.   Name 8 rays using the figure in #10.

16.   Name 4 segments using the figure in #11.

17.   Name 10 segments using the figure in #12.

Name _____   Date _____

Classifying Angles

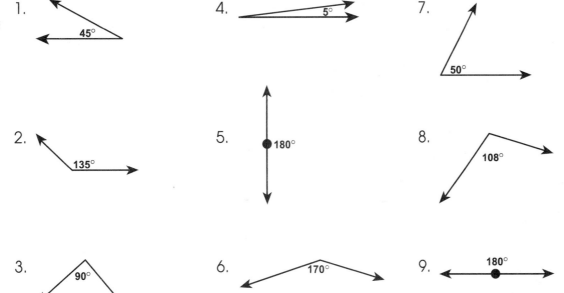

Acute	Right	Obtuse	Straight
$\angle 0° \; x \; \angle 90°$	$x = 90°$	$90° \angle x \angle 180°$	$x = 180°$

1.

45°

4.

5°

7.

50°

2.

135°

5. ●180°

8.

108°

3.

90°

6.

170°

9. ← 180° ● →

Figure 1

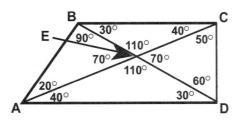

10. List 5 acute angles.

11. List 2 right angles.

12. List 2 obtuse angles.

13. List 2 straight angles.

Figure 2

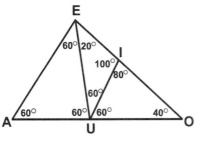

14. List 5 acute angles.

15. List 2 obtuse angles.

16. List 2 straight angles.

Name _____   Date _____

Flying High

Use a ruler and protractor.

1. Locate point A 1 in. from the bottom and 1 in. from the right side of the page.

2. Draw segment AB $\frac{3}{4}$ in. long parallel to the bottom of the page so B is $1\frac{3}{4}$ in. from the right side of the page.

3. Draw segment BC 1 in. long and m∠ABC is 150°. (C is above segment AB.)

4. Draw segment CD 1 in. long and m∠BCD is 150°. (D is above segment BC.)

5. Draw segment DE 2 in. long and m∠CDE is 150°. (E is on the same side of segment CD as B.)

6. Draw segment EF $\frac{1}{2}$ in. long and m∠DEF is 100°. (F and B are on opposite sides of segment DE.)

7. Draw segment FG $\frac{1}{2}$ in. long and m∠EFG is 90°. (G and E are on opposite sides of segment CD.)

8. Connect G to D, G to E, and F to D.

9. Draw segments BH and BJ 1/2 in. long and m∠ABH and m∠ABJ are 90°.

10. Draw segments BK and BL 1/2 in. long and m∠CBK and m∠CBL are 90°. (H is on the same side of segment AB as K.)

11. Connect H to K and Connect J to L.

12. Draw segments CM and CN $\frac{1}{2}$ in. long and m∠BCM and m∠BCN are 90°.

13. Draw segments CO and CP $\frac{1}{2}$ in. long and m∠DCO and m∠DCP are 90°. (M is on the same side of segment BS as O.)

14. Connect M to O and connect N to P.

0-7424-1777-8 *Intro to Geometry*

Name _____ Date _____

Congruence and Addition Properties of Angles

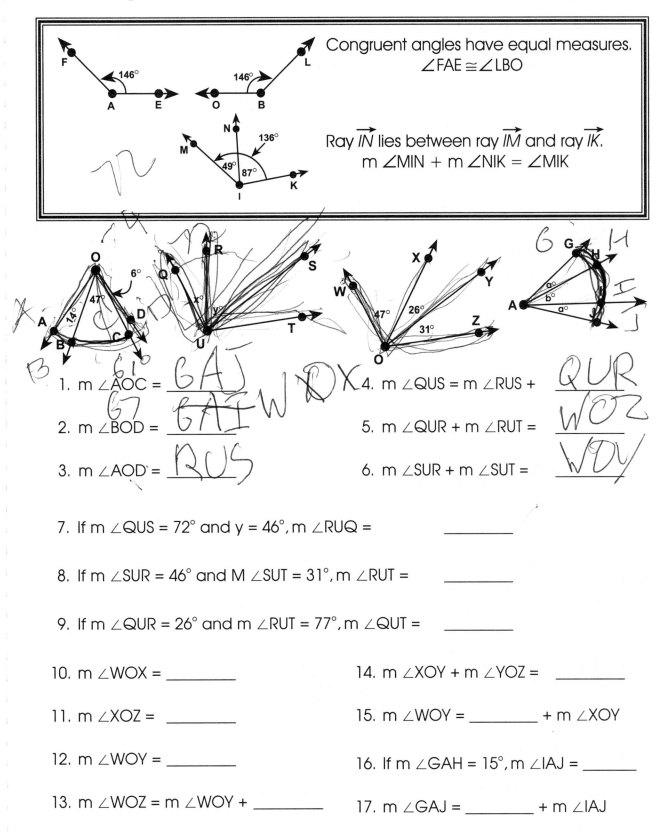

Congruent angles have equal measures.
∠FAE ≅ ∠LBO

Ray $\overrightarrow{IN}$ lies between ray $\overrightarrow{IM}$ and ray $\overrightarrow{IK}$.
m ∠MIN + m ∠NIK = ∠MIK

1. m ∠AOC = _____
2. m ∠BOD = _____
3. m ∠AOD = _____

4. m ∠QUS = m ∠RUS + _____
5. m ∠QUR + m ∠RUT = _____
6. m ∠SUR + m ∠SUT = _____

7. If m ∠QUS = 72° and y = 46°, m ∠RUQ = _____

8. If m ∠SUR = 46° and M ∠SUT = 31°, m ∠RUT = _____

9. If m ∠QUR = 26° and m ∠RUT = 77°, m ∠QUT = _____

10. m ∠WOX = _____

11. m ∠XOZ = _____

12. m ∠WOY = _____

13. m ∠WOZ = m ∠WOY + _____

14. m ∠XOY + m ∠YOZ = _____

15. m ∠WOY = _____ + m ∠XOY

16. If m ∠GAH = 15°, m ∠IAJ = _____

17. m ∠GAJ = _____ + m ∠IAJ

Special Pairs of Angles

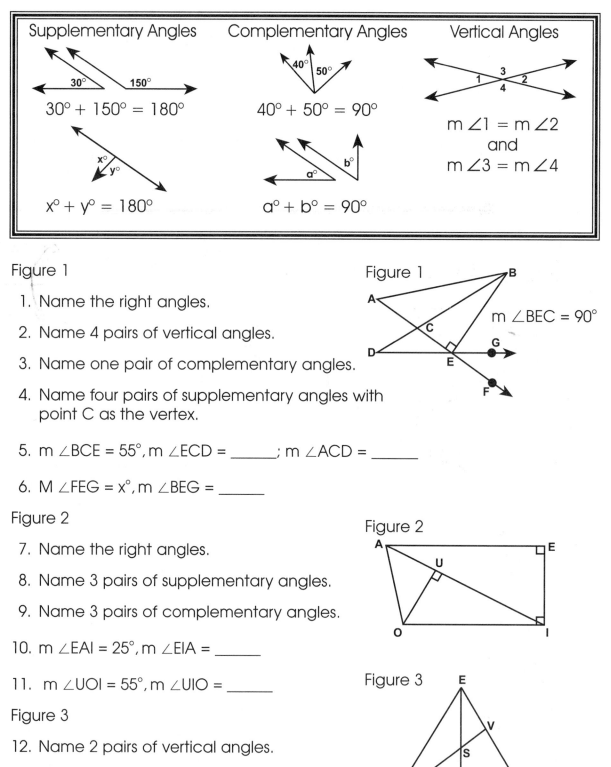

Supplementary Angles

$30° + 150° = 180°$

$x° + y° = 180°$

Complementary Angles

$40° + 50° = 90°$

$a° + b° = 90°$

Vertical Angles

$m \angle 1 = m \angle 2$
and
$m \angle 3 = m \angle 4$

Figure 1

1. Name the right angles.

2. Name 4 pairs of vertical angles.

3. Name one pair of complementary angles.

4. Name four pairs of supplementary angles with point C as the vertex.

5. $m \angle BCE = 55°, m \angle ECD =$ _____ ; $m \angle ACD =$ _____

6. $M \angle FEG = x°, m \angle BEG =$ _____

Figure 1

$m \angle BEC = 90°$

Figure 2

7. Name the right angles.

8. Name 3 pairs of supplementary angles.

9. Name 3 pairs of complementary angles.

10. $m \angle EAI = 25°, m \angle EIA =$ _____

11. $m \angle UOI = 55°, m \angle UIO =$ _____

Figure 3

12. Name 2 pairs of vertical angles.

13. Name 2 pairs of supplementary angles.

Figure 2

Figure 3

Name _____ Date _____

Practice with Special Angles

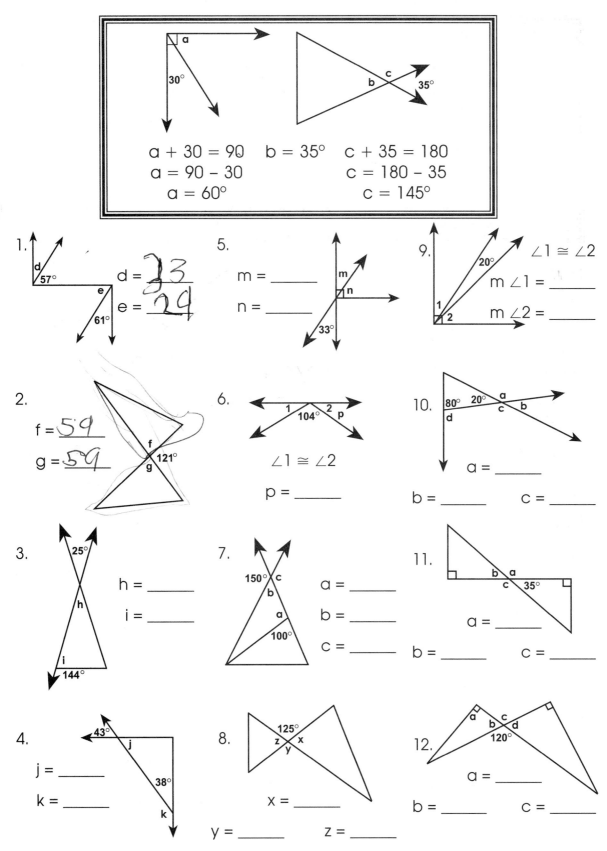

a + 30 = 90   b = 35°   c + 35 = 180
a = 90 − 30   c = 180 − 35
a = 60°   c = 145°

1.
d = 33
e = 24

5.
m = _____
n = _____

9.
∠1 ≅ ∠2
m ∠1 = _____
m ∠2 = _____

2.
f = 59
g = 59

6.
∠1 ≅ ∠2
p = _____

10.
a = _____
b = _____   c = _____

3.
h = _____
i = _____

7.
a = _____
b = _____
c = _____

11.
a = _____
b = _____   c = _____

4.
j = _____
k = _____

8.
x = _____
y = _____   z = _____

12.
a = _____
b = _____   c = _____

...More Practice with Special Angles

Find x and the measure of the angles.

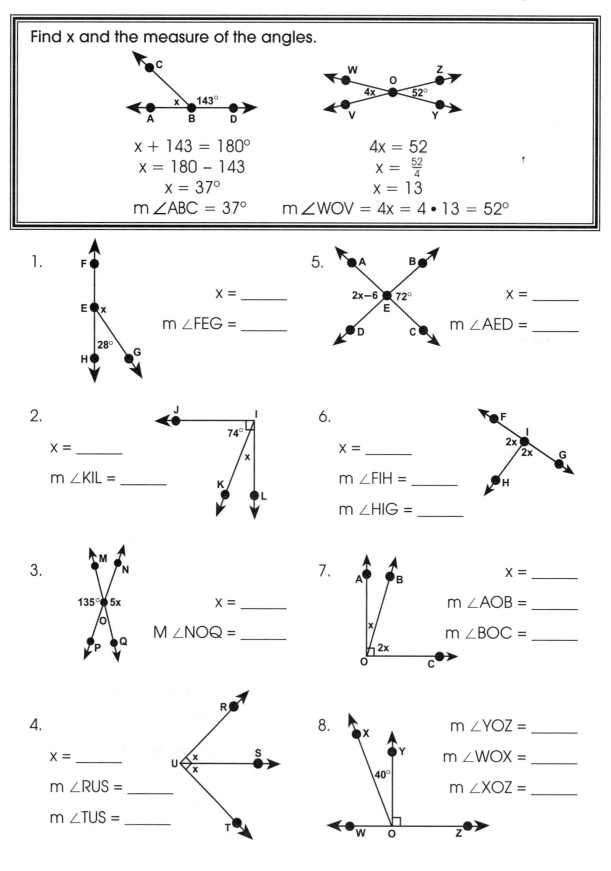

$x + 143 = 180°$
$x = 180 - 143$
$x = 37°$
$m\angle ABC = 37°$

$4x = 52$
$x = \frac{52}{4}$
$x = 13$
$m\angle WOV = 4x = 4 \cdot 13 = 52°$

1.   X = _____

m ∠FEG = _____

5.   X = _____

m ∠AED = _____

2.   X = _____

m ∠KIL = _____

6.   X = _____

m ∠FIH = _____

m ∠HIG = _____

3.   X = _____

M ∠NOQ = _____

7.   X = _____

m ∠AOB = _____

m ∠BOC = _____

4.   X = _____

m ∠RUS = _____

m ∠TUS = _____

8.   m ∠YOZ = _____

m ∠WOX = _____

m ∠XOZ = _____

More Than Meets the Eye — Fun and Games

1. Remove three pieces to leave three squares.

2. Remove six pieces to leave three squares.

3. How many triangles are in the figure?

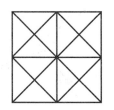

4. How many triangles are in the figure?

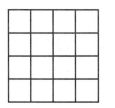

5. How many squares are in the figure?

6. How many squares are in the figure?

Just For Fun

Determine the number of cubes in each figure. The figures are symmetrical.
If a cube is left out in the base, it is left out all the way through the design.

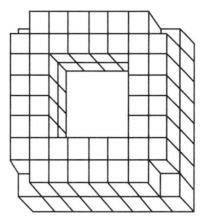

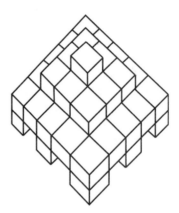

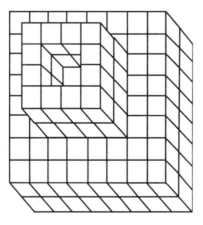

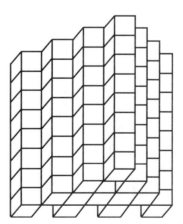

Name _____   Date _____

Classifying Triangles by Sides

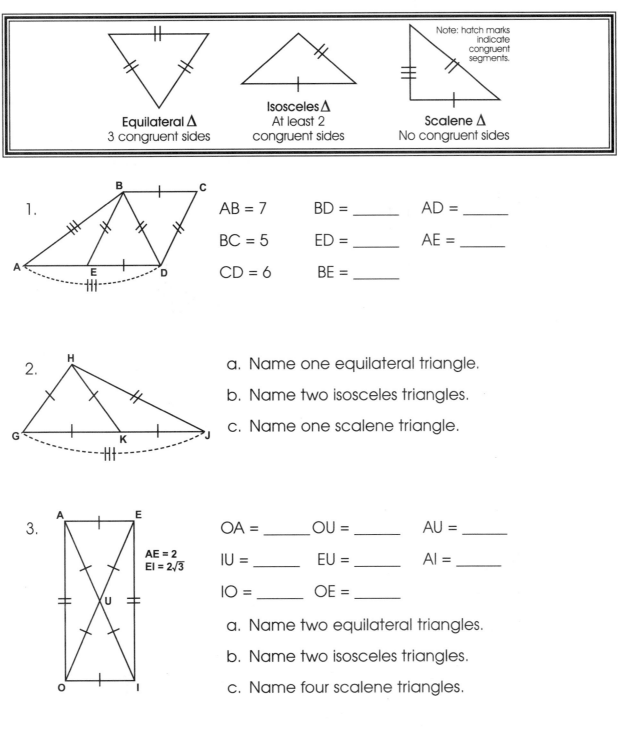

Equilateral △
3 congruent sides

Isosceles △
At least 2
congruent sides

Scalene △
No congruent sides

Note: hatch marks
indicate
congruent
segments.

1.

AB = 7   BD = _____   AD = _____

BC = 5   ED = _____   AE = _____

CD = 6   BE = _____

2.

a. Name one equilateral triangle.

b. Name two isosceles triangles.

c. Name one scalene triangle.

3.

AE = 2
EI = 2√3

OA = _____   OU = _____   AU = _____

IU = _____   EU = _____   AI = _____

IO = _____   OE = _____

a. Name two equilateral triangles.

b. Name two isosceles triangles.

c. Name four scalene triangles.

Classify the triangles having sides as indicated.

4. 9, 2, 8   5. 5, 6, 5   6. 4.5, 4.5, 4.5   7. 7, 6.9, .7

Name _____   Date _____

Classifying Triangles by Angles

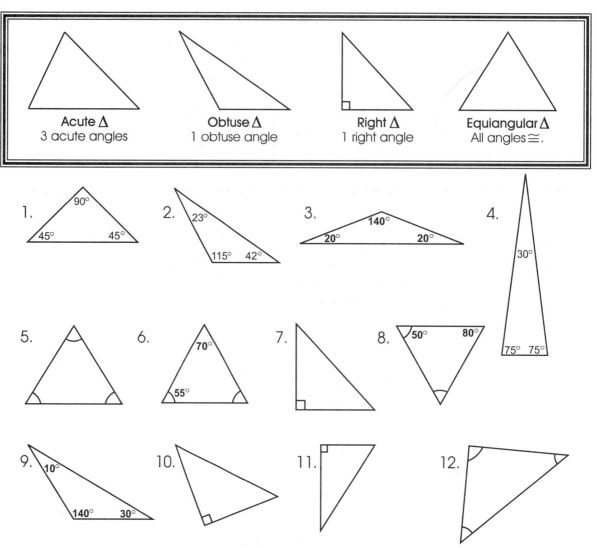

True or False

13. All equilateral triangles are isosceles triangles.

14. Some scalene triangles are isosceles triangles.

15. A right triangle may be an isosceles triangle.

16. Every equiangular triangle is an acute triangle.

17. An obtuse triangle has two acute angles.

18. Some acute triangles are equiangular.

19. A right triangle is also an equiangular triangle.

20. Some isosceles triangles are acute.

Name _____   Date _____

Interior Angles of a Triangle

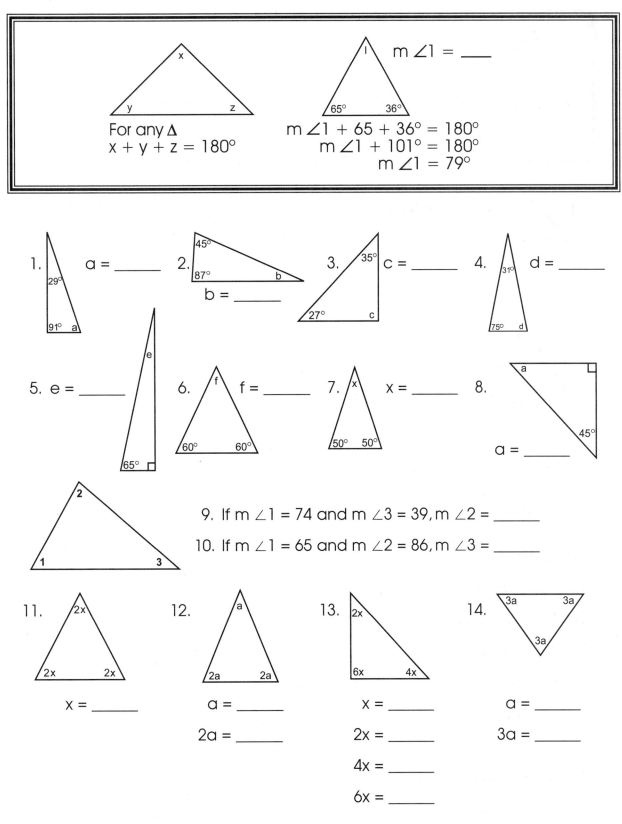

For any Δ
$x + y + z = 180°$

$m\angle 1 = $ ___

$m\angle 1 + 65 + 36° = 180°$
$m\angle 1 + 101° = 180°$
$m\angle 1 = 79°$

1. a = _____

2. b = _____

3. c = _____

4. d = _____

5. e = _____

6. f = _____

7. x = _____

8. a = _____

9. If $m\angle 1 = 74$ and $m\angle 3 = 39$, $m\angle 2 = $ _____

10. If $m\angle 1 = 65$ and $m\angle 2 = 86$, $m\angle 3 = $ _____

11. x = _____

12. a = _____

    2a = _____

13. x = _____

    2x = _____

    4x = _____

    6x = _____

14. a = _____

    3a = _____

Name _____   Date _____

Exterior and Interior Angles of a Triangle

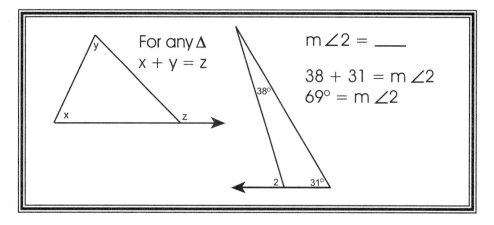

Find the measures of the angles indicated.

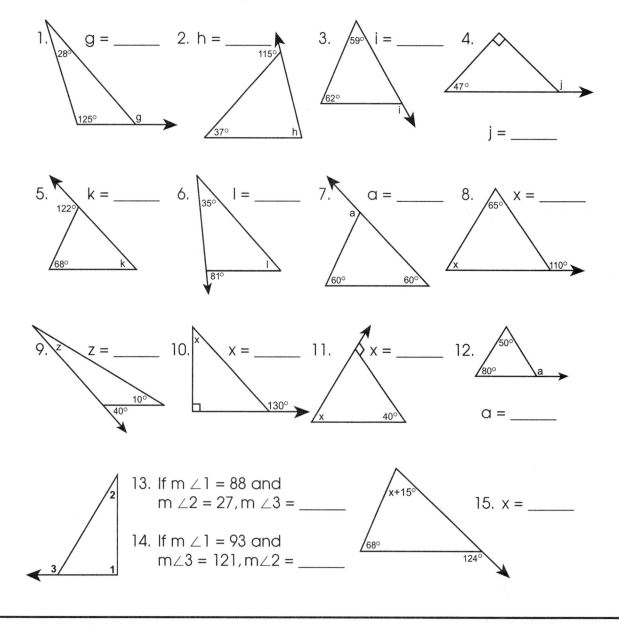

1. g = _____
2. h = _____
3. i = _____
4. j = _____

5. k = _____
6. l = _____
7. a = _____
8. x = _____

9. z = _____
10. x = _____
11. x = _____
12. a = _____

13. If m ∠1 = 88 and m ∠2 = 27, m ∠3 = _____

14. If m ∠1 = 93 and m∠3 = 121, m∠2 = _____

15. x = _____

Name _____ Date _____

Angles

The three angles of a triangle total 180°.
Two adjacent angles that form a straight line total 180°.

Determine the measure of each indicated angle in the diagram below. Do not use a protractor.

A. _____   I. _____   Q. __55°_____

B. _____   J. __60°_____   R. _____

C. _____   K. _____   S. _____

D. _____   L. _____   T. _____

E. _____   M. _____   U. _____

F. _____   N. _____   V. _____

G. _____   O. _____   W. _____

H. _____   P. _____   X. __25°_____

Find the sum of all the angles. _____

How is the product 6 x 360° related to the angle sum? _____

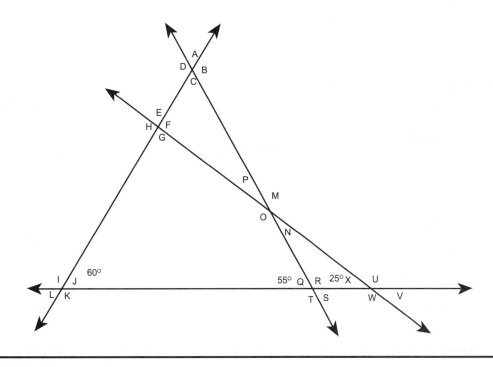

Name _____   Date _____

Triangle Try Outs

> **Triangle Inequality** states that the sum of any two sides of a triangle is greater than the length of the third side.

1. On a separate sheet, try to draw triangles with the given side lengths.

   A. 2 in., 3 in., 5 in.   B. 2 in., 3 in., 4 in.   C. 2 in., 5 in., 5 in.   D. 2 in., 5 in., 8 in.

2. Which triangle(s) were you able to draw? _____ Why? _____

Write *yes* or *no* to indicate if the three given lengths can be the sides of a triangle.

3. 8 cm, 3 cm, 4 cm   _____   5. 5 m, 7 m, 7 m   _____

4. 3 cm, 5 cm, 7 cm   _____   6. 6.2 m, 7.1 m, 12.6 m   _____

7. On a separate sheet, use a protractor and try to draw triangles with the given angle measures.

   E. 30°, 90°, 60°   F. 20°, 40°, 40°   G. 140°, 20°, 20°   H. 40°, 40°, 40°

8. Which triangle(s) were you able to draw? _____ Why? _____

9. The angle sum of any triangle is _____.

Consider the triangle shown.

10. Which angle appears to be the largest? _____ the smallest? _____

11. Which side appears to be the longest? _____ the shortest? _____

12. In a triangle, the longest side is opposite the _____ angle.

For each triangle, list the sides of the triangle from shortest to longest.

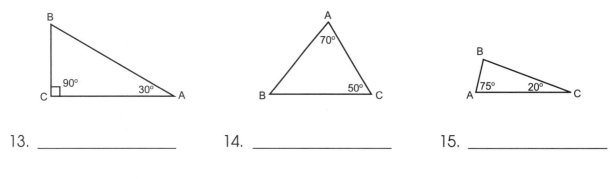

13. _____   14. _____   15. _____

Two Triangle Inequality

Given that two sides of one triangle are congruent to two sides of a second triangle and the included angle of the first triangle is smaller than the included angle of the second triangle, then the third side of the first triangle is smaller than the third side of the second triangle.

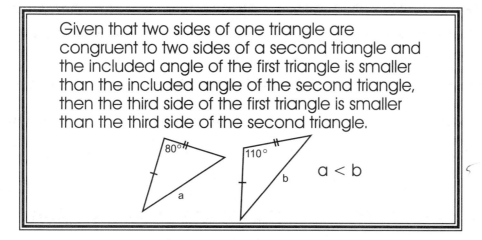

$a < b$

List the labeled sides from shortest to longest.

1.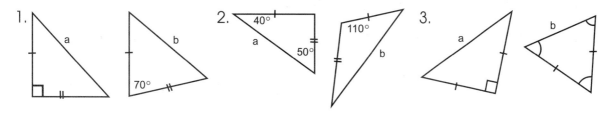

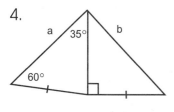

2.

3.

4.

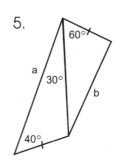

5.

6.

7.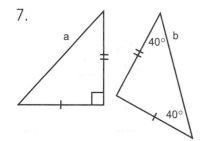

8.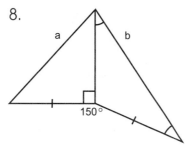

9.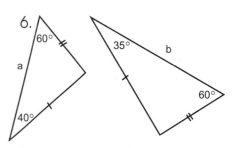

Squares and Square Roots

$x^2 = x \cdot x$ $\sqrt{x^2} = \sqrt{x \cdot x} = x$ $\sqrt{50} = \sqrt{2 \cdot 5 \cdot 5} = 5\sqrt{2}$

$6^2 = 6 \cdot 6 = 36$ $\sqrt{49} = \sqrt{7 \cdot 7} = 7$ $\sqrt{300} = \sqrt{2 \cdot 2 \cdot 3 \cdot 5 \cdot 5}$

$15^2 = 15 \cdot 15 = 225$ $\sqrt{400} = \sqrt{20^2} = 20$ $= 2 \cdot 5\sqrt{3}$

                                                                 $= 10\sqrt{3}$

Find the indicated squares.

1. 11^2 2. 8^2 3. 4^2 4. $(\frac{1}{2})^2$

5. 1.1^2 6. 1^2 7. 5^2 8. 6^2

9. 2.3^2 10. 1.2^2 11. $(\frac{2}{3})^2$ 12. $(\frac{1}{4})^2$

Find the indicated square roots.

13. $\sqrt{4}$ 14. $\sqrt{81}$ 15. $\sqrt{100}$ 16. $\sqrt{64}$

17. $\sqrt{121}$ 18. $\sqrt{25}$ 19. $\sqrt{9}$ 20. $\sqrt{49}$

21. $\sqrt{16}$ 22. $\sqrt{1.44}$ 23. $\sqrt{\frac{1}{9}}$ 24. $\sqrt{\frac{4}{25}}$

Simplify each of the following. Circle the answer in each row of problems that does not belong. Write the corresponding letter above the problem number below.

25. N	$\sqrt{200}$	L	$4\sqrt{50}$	S	$2\sqrt{50}$	
26. T	$\sqrt{720}$	A	$12\sqrt{60}$	Q	$4\sqrt{45}$	
27. R	$10\sqrt{45}$	M	$3\sqrt{50}$	P	$\sqrt{450}$	
28. Q	$\sqrt{180}$	A	$3\sqrt{20}$	I	$2\sqrt{60}$	
29. U	$2\sqrt{32}$	D	$\sqrt{96}$	W	$4\sqrt{8}$	
30. C	$3\sqrt{18}$	E	$\sqrt{216}$	R	$2\sqrt{54}$	

A $\sqrt{}$ is truly   ___ ___ ___ ___ ___ ___ ___ !

                         27   26   29   28   30   26   25

Name _____   Date _____

Right Triangles

For any right Δ
$a^2 + b^2 = c^2$
(Pythagorean Theorem)

$c = $ ___

$3^2 + 4^2 = c^2$
$9 + 16 = c^2$
$25 = c^2$
$5 = c$

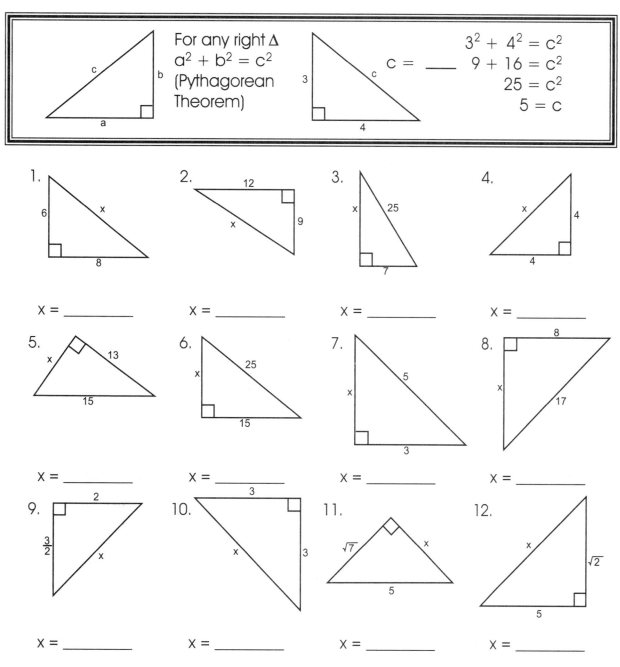

1.

6, x, 8

X = _____

2.

12, x, 9

X = _____

3.

x, 25, 7

X = _____

4.

x, 4, 4

X = _____

5.

x, 13, 15

X = _____

6.

x, 25, 15

X = _____

7.

x, 5, 3

X = _____

8.

8, x, 17

X = _____

9.

2, $\frac{3}{2}$, x

X = _____

10.

3, x, 3

X = _____

11.

$\sqrt{7}$, x, 5

X = _____

12.

x, $\sqrt{2}$, 5

X = _____

13. To go from Dukeville to Karlton, you can travel along the two main highways or the direct route along Valley Road.

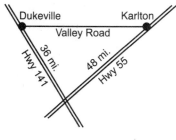

a. How long is the highway route?

b. How long is the Valley Road route?

c. How many miles do you save by taking the direct route?

Name _____   Date _____

Special Right Triangles

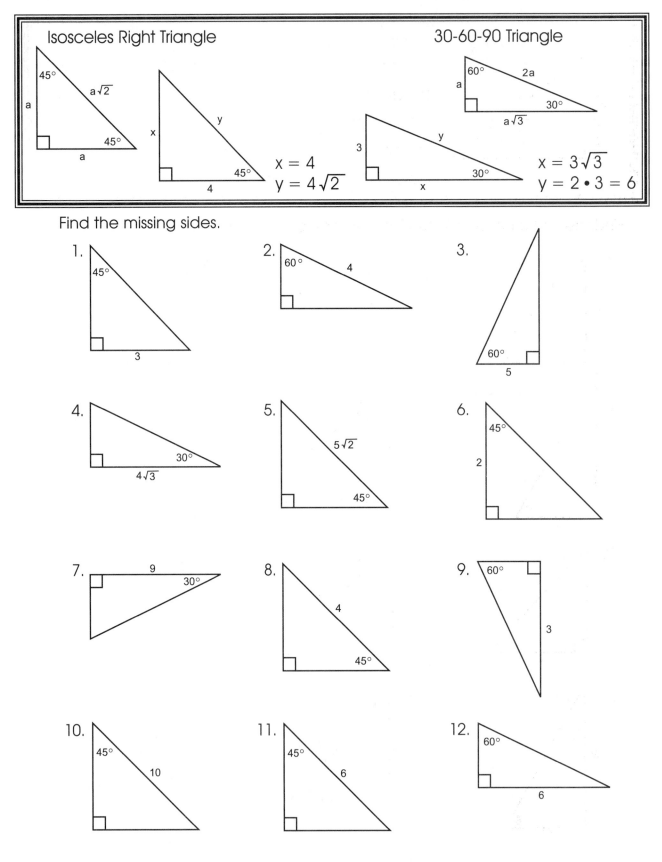

Isosceles Right Triangle

30-60-90 Triangle

$x = 4$
$y = 4\sqrt{2}$

$x = 3\sqrt{3}$
$y = 2 \cdot 3 = 6$

Find the missing sides.

1. 45°, 3

2. 60°, 4

3. 60°, 5

4. 30°, $4\sqrt{3}$

5. $5\sqrt{2}$, 45°

6. 45°, 2

7. 9, 30°

8. 4, 45°

9. 60°, 3

10. 45°, 10

11. 45°, 6

12. 60°, 6

Name _____   Date _____

Right Triangle Trigonometry

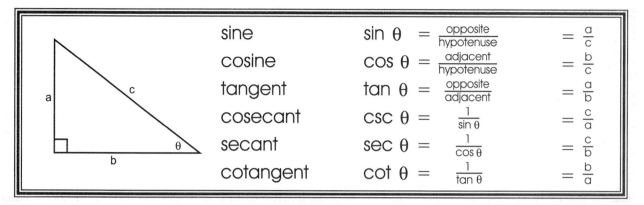

sine	$\sin \theta = \dfrac{\text{opposite}}{\text{hypotenuse}}$	$= \dfrac{a}{c}$
cosine	$\cos \theta = \dfrac{\text{adjacent}}{\text{hypotenuse}}$	$= \dfrac{b}{c}$
tangent	$\tan \theta = \dfrac{\text{opposite}}{\text{adjacent}}$	$= \dfrac{a}{b}$
cosecant	$\csc \theta = \dfrac{1}{\sin \theta}$	$= \dfrac{c}{a}$
secant	$\sec \theta = \dfrac{1}{\cos \theta}$	$= \dfrac{c}{b}$
cotangent	$\cot \theta = \dfrac{1}{\tan \theta}$	$= \dfrac{b}{a}$

Find the six trigonometric functions for the angles below.

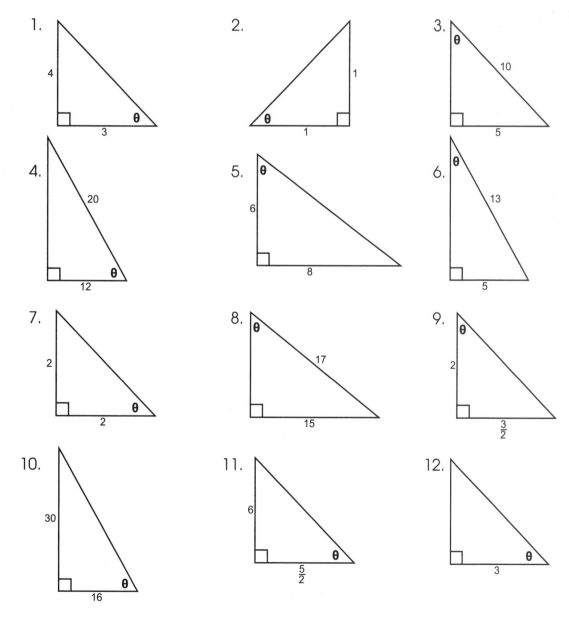

Transformations

Three Basic Movements

1. Translation (Slide) 2. Rotation (Turn) 3. Reflection (Flip)

Which single basic motion will make these figures coincide?

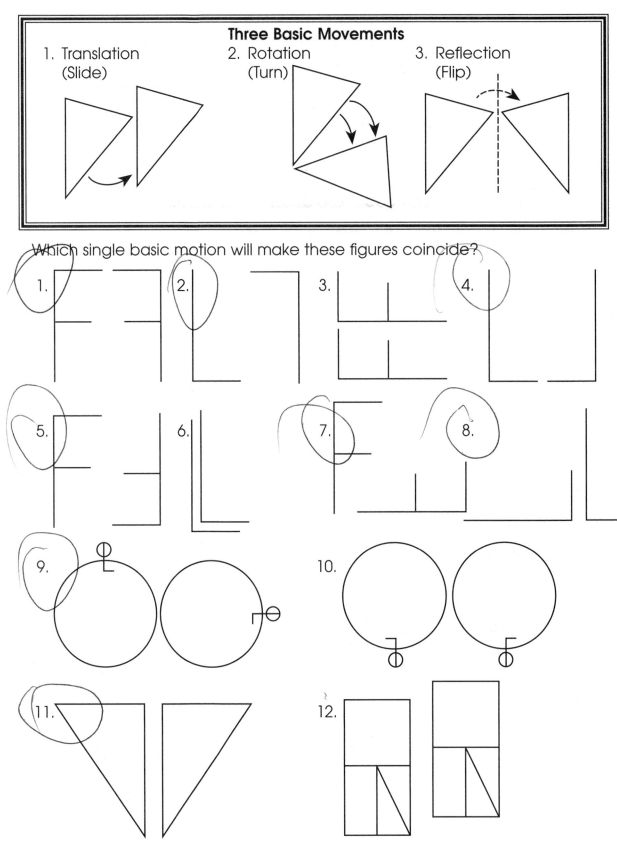

1.

2.

3.

4.

5.

6.

7.

8.

9.

10.

11.

12.

Sketching Transformations

Slip Sliding Away...

Sketch a translation of each figure.

One good turn deserves another...

Rotate these figures to the indicated positions.

$\frac{1}{4}$
Turn Left

Original Figure

$\frac{1}{2}$
Turn Right

Mirror, Mirror On the Wall...

Find the reflection of each picture across the given line.

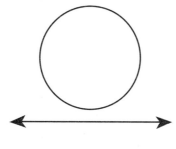

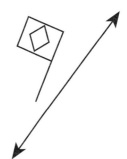

Name _____ Date _____

Parts of Congruent Triangles

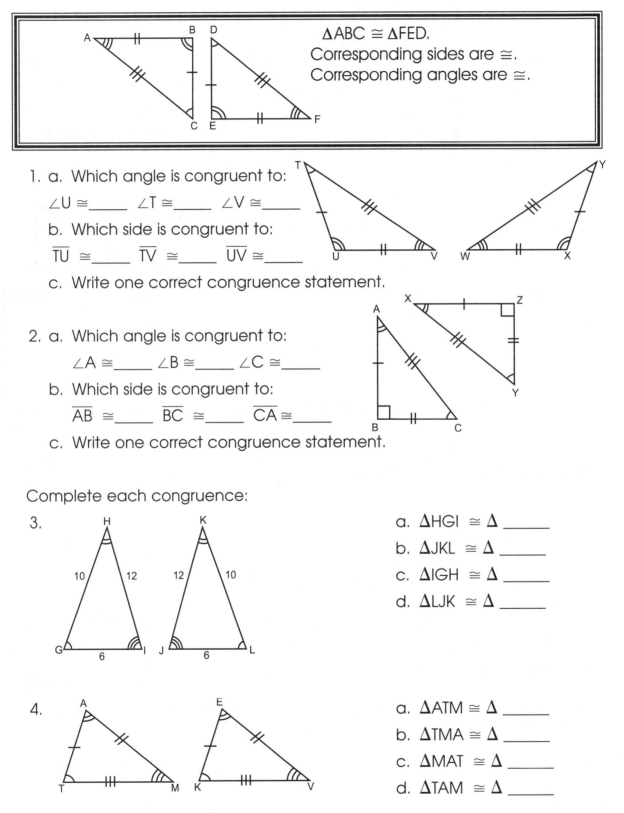

△ABC ≅ △FED.
Corresponding sides are ≅.
Corresponding angles are ≅.

1. a. Which angle is congruent to:

   ∠U ≅ _____ ∠T ≅ _____ ∠V ≅ _____

   b. Which side is congruent to:

   $\overline{TU}$ ≅ _____ $\overline{TV}$ ≅ _____ $\overline{UV}$ ≅ _____

   c. Write one correct congruence statement.

2. a. Which angle is congruent to:

   ∠A ≅ _____ ∠B ≅ _____ ∠C ≅ _____

   b. Which side is congruent to:

   $\overline{AB}$ ≅ _____ $\overline{BC}$ ≅ _____ $\overline{CA}$ ≅ _____

   c. Write one correct congruence statement.

Complete each congruence:

3.

   a. △HGI ≅ △ _____
   b. △JKL ≅ △ _____
   c. △IGH ≅ △ _____
   d. △LJK ≅ △ _____

4.

   a. △ATM ≅ △ _____
   b. △TMA ≅ △ _____
   c. △MAT ≅ △ _____
   d. △TAM ≅ △ _____

Congruent Triangles: ASA and AAS

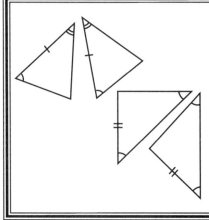

ASA — Angle, Side, Angle
two angles and the included side of one triangle are congruent to the corresponding parts of another triangle → ≅ △s

AAS — Angle, Angle, Side
two angles and the non-included side of one triangle are congruent to the corresponding parts of another triangle → ≅ △s

State whether these pairs of triangles are congruent by ASA or AAS. If neither method works, write N.

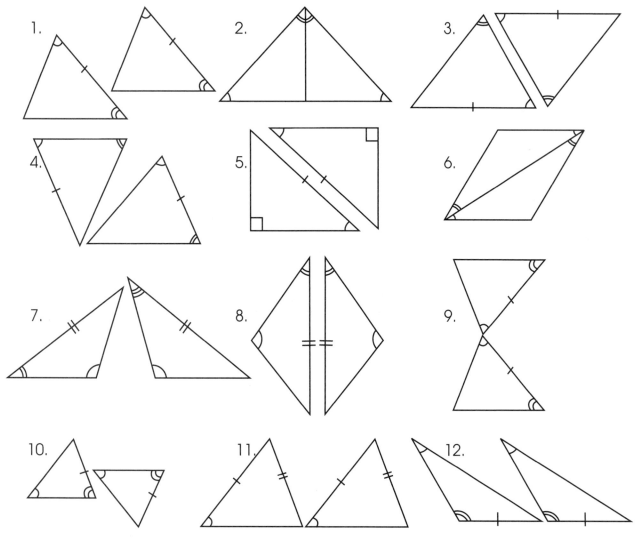

Congruent Triangles: HL

HL — Hypotenuse, Leg
the hypotenuse and a leg of one right triangle
are congruent to the corresponding parts of
another triangle ⟶ ≅ △s

State whether these pairs of triangles are congruent by HL. If not, write N.

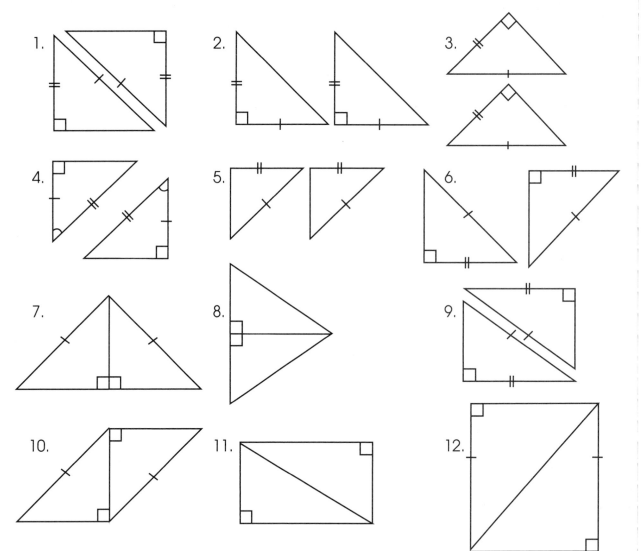

1.   2.   3.

4.   5.   6.

7.   8.   9.

10.   11.   12.

Triangle Congruence

State whether these pairs of triangles are congruent by SSS, SAS, ASA, AAS, or HL. If none of these methods work, write N.

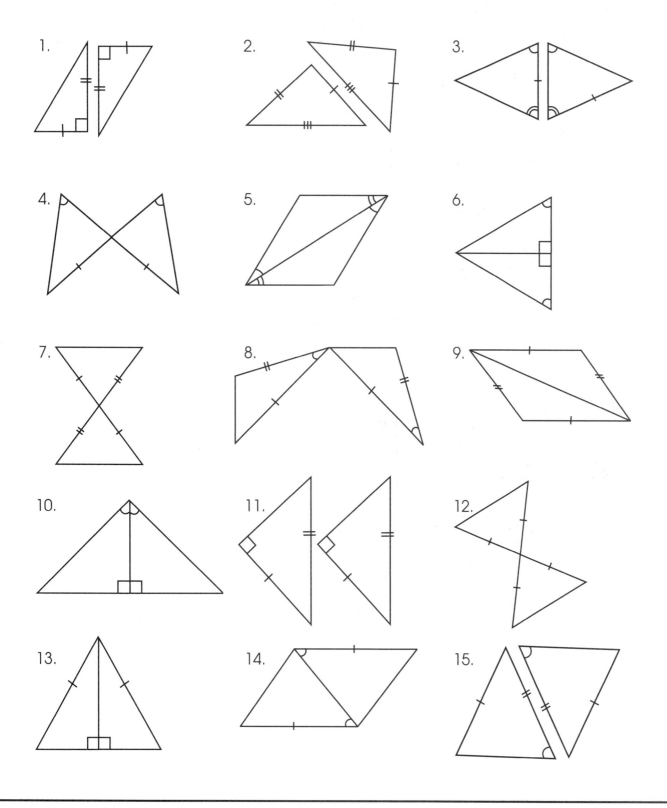

Name _____   Date _____

Isosceles Triangle Properties

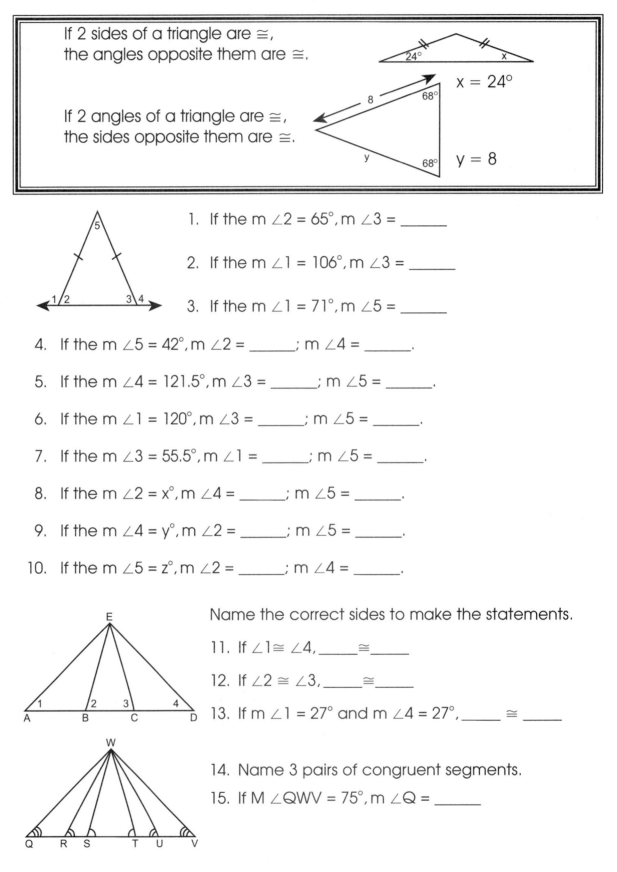

If 2 sides of a triangle are ≅,
the angles opposite them are ≅.

$x = 24°$

If 2 angles of a triangle are ≅,
the sides opposite them are ≅.

$y = 8$

1. If the m ∠2 = 65°, m ∠3 = _____

2. If the m ∠1 = 106°, m ∠3 = _____

3. If the m ∠1 = 71°, m ∠5 = _____

4. If the m ∠5 = 42°, m ∠2 = _____; m ∠4 = _____.

5. If the m ∠4 = 121.5°, m ∠3 = _____; m ∠5 = _____.

6. If the m ∠1 = 120°, m ∠3 = _____; m ∠5 = _____.

7. If the m ∠3 = 55.5°, m ∠1 = _____; m ∠5 = _____.

8. If the m ∠2 = x°, m ∠4 = _____; m ∠5 = _____.

9. If the m ∠4 = y°, m ∠2 = _____; m ∠5 = _____.

10. If the m ∠5 = z°, m ∠2 = _____; m ∠4 = _____.

Name the correct sides to make the statements.

11. If ∠1 ≅ ∠4, _____ ≅ _____

12. If ∠2 ≅ ∠3, _____ ≅ _____

13. If m ∠1 = 27° and m ∠4 = 27°, _____ ≅ _____

14. Name 3 pairs of congruent segments.

15. If M ∠QWV = 75°, m ∠Q = _____

Ratio and Proportion

Change each ratio to a fraction in simplest form.

5 out of 7 children	15 to 20	2 : 6
$\frac{5}{7}$	$\frac{15}{20} = \frac{3}{4}$	$\frac{2}{6} = \frac{1}{3}$

1. 3 to 15

2. 16 to 4

3. 18 out of 27

4. 64 : 48

5. 4 to 20

6. 12 out of 30

7. 72 : 60

8. 8xy : 6 yz

9. 125ab : 200bc

Solve each of the following proportions.

$$\frac{3}{4} = \frac{9}{x} \rightarrow 3x = 4 \bullet 9 \rightarrow 3x = 36 \rightarrow 3x \div 3 = 36 \div 3 \rightarrow x = 12$$

$$\frac{1}{2} = \frac{y}{7} \rightarrow 2y = 1 \bullet 7 \rightarrow 2y = 7 \rightarrow 2y \div 2 = 7 \div 2 \rightarrow y = 3.5$$

10. $\frac{x}{6} = \frac{8}{3}$

11. $\frac{x}{10} = \frac{6}{5}$

12. $\frac{3}{x} = \frac{7}{5}$

13. $\frac{4}{11} = \frac{x}{2}$

14. 6 : x = 3 : 7

15. x : 9 = 7 : 3

16. 5 : 6 = x : 30

17. 3 : 8 = 27 : x

18. 4 : 5 = x : 30

$$\frac{AD}{DB} = \frac{AE}{EC}$$

Find the missing length.

19. AD = 2   DB = 4   AE = 3   EC = _____

20. DB = 5   EC = 7   AD = 3   AE = _____

21. AD = 4   AE = 5   EC = 10   DB = _____

22. AD = 5   AB = 8   AE = 4   EC = _____

Name _____   Date _____

Geometric Ratios and Proportions

Use ratios and proportions to solve the following problems.

1. On a map with the legend 2 in. = 50 miles, two cities are 7 in. apart. What is the actual distance between the two cities?

2. Susan is having a 3" x 5" photograph enlarged so that the width is $16\frac{1}{2}$". What is the length of the enlargement?

3. Amy must depict a 12' wide x 15' long room on a drawing that is 18" wide. What is the length of the drawing?

4. Eli is drawing a floor plan (1" = 2') of his room. His desk measures 24" x 36". What are the floor plan dimensions of his desk?

5. Kyle wants to reduce an 8" x 10" photograph so it fits in a 3" x 5" frame. What are the largest dimensions he can use?

Write the following ratios. Compute the quotients to the nearest hundredth.

6. Your height/distance from waist to floor _____/_____ = _____

7. Shoulder to fingertip/elbow to fingertip _____/_____ = _____

8. Middle segment of finger/end segment of finger _____/_____ = _____

The golden ratio is the ratio of the length to the width of a golden rectangle, which equals approximately 1.61/1. Leonardo da Vinci used the golden ratio in his drawings of human bodies.

9. How do you measure up? Which of the ratios of questions 6-8 are close to the golden ratio? _____

10. Photographs are often 8" x 10", 5" x 8", and 3" x 5". Find the length/width ratio of each size. _____ Which size most closely approximates the golden ratio? _____.

(INSERT AN ILLUSTRATION)

Similar Triangles

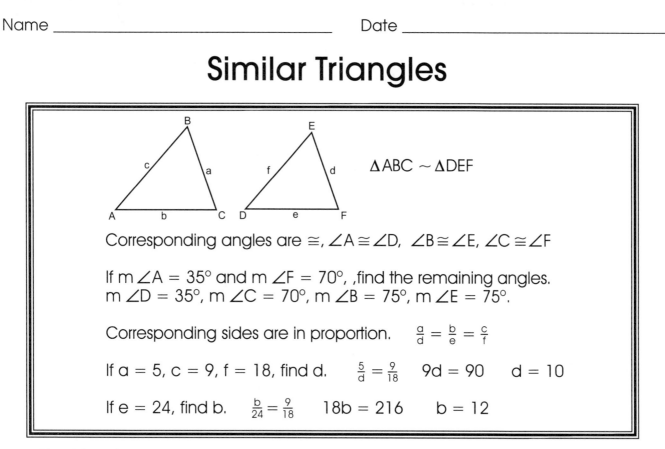

$\triangle ABC \sim \triangle DEF$

Corresponding angles are $\cong$, $\angle A \cong \angle D$, $\angle B \cong \angle E$, $\angle C \cong \angle F$

If m $\angle A = 35°$ and m $\angle F = 70°$, find the remaining angles.
m $\angle D = 35°$, m $\angle C = 70°$, m $\angle B = 75°$, m $\angle E = 75°$.

Corresponding sides are in proportion. $\frac{a}{d} = \frac{b}{e} = \frac{c}{f}$

If a = 5, c = 9, f = 18, find d. $\frac{5}{d} = \frac{9}{18}$ $9d = 90$ $d = 10$

If e = 24, find b. $\frac{b}{24} = \frac{9}{18}$ $18b = 216$ $b = 12$

The triangles are similar as they appear. Find the measure of angles 1-23.

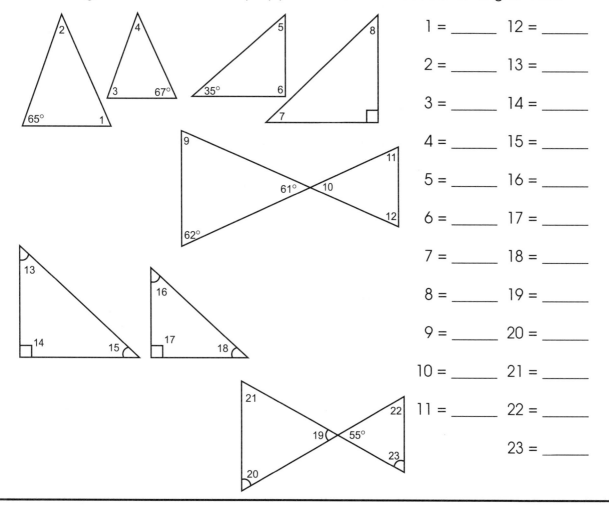

1 = _____   12 = _____

2 = _____   13 = _____

3 = _____   14 = _____

4 = _____   15 = _____

5 = _____   16 = _____

6 = _____   17 = _____

7 = _____   18 = _____

8 = _____   19 = _____

9 = _____   20 = _____

10 = _____   21 = _____

11 = _____   22 = _____

23 = _____

Similar Triangles

Find the lengths of sides a-f.

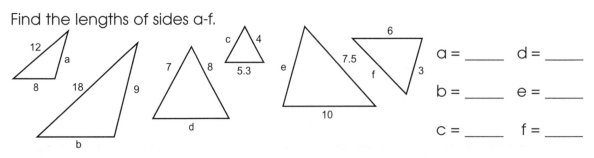

a = _____ d = _____

b = _____ e = _____

c = _____ f = _____

Find each missing measure. The triangles are similar as they appear.

1. 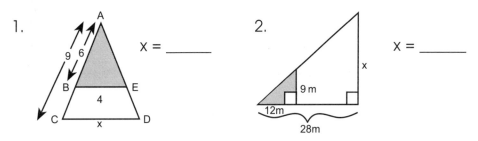 X = _____

2. 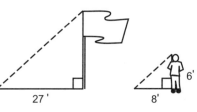 X = _____

3. A flagpole casts a shadow 27 feet long. A person standing nearby casts a shadow 8 feet long. If the person is 6 feet tall, how tall is the flagpole?

4. Christopher wants to reduce a triangular pattern with sides 16, 16 and 20 centimeters. If the longest side of the new pattern is to be 15 centimeters, how long should the other 2 sides be?

5. A 9 foot ladder leans against a building 7 feet above the ground. At what height would a 15 foot ladder touch the building if both ladders form the same angle with the ground?

6. A flagpole casts a shadow 24 feet long. A flower standing nearby casts a shadow 3 feet long. If the flagpole is 12 feet tall, how tall is the flower?

7. Sam wants to enlarge a triangle with sides 3, 6 and 6 inches. If the shortest side of the new triangle is 13 inches, how long will the other two sides be?

8. A 6 foot ladder leans against a building 4 feet above the ground. At what height would a 15 foot ladder touch the building if both ladders form the same angle with the ground?

Identifying Similar Triangles

AA – Angle, Angle

2 angles of one triangle ≅ to 2 angles of another.

Find the missing angle measures. Then, tell whether the triangles are similar by the AA Property.

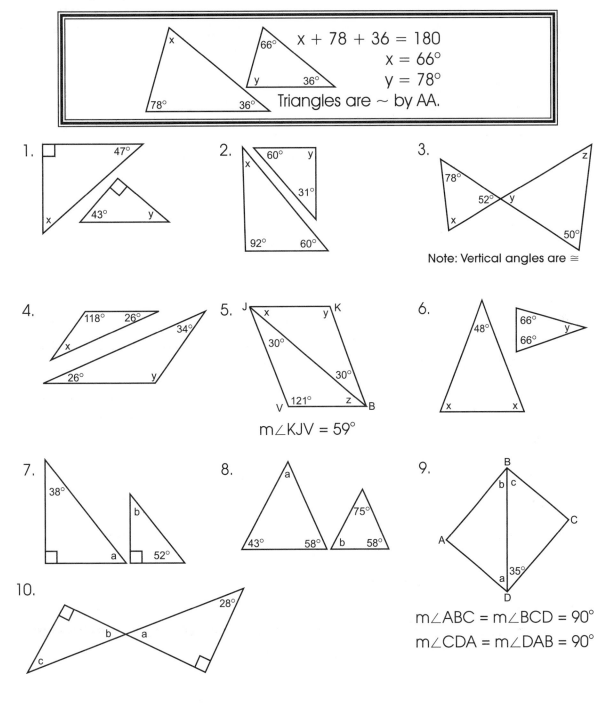

x + 78 + 36 = 180
x = 66°
y = 78°
Triangles are ~ by AA.

3. Note: Vertical angles are ≅

5. m∠KJV = 59°

9. m∠ABC = m∠BCD = 90°
m∠CDA = m∠DAB = 90°

Identifying Similar Triangles

SAS–Side, Angle, Side
2 pairs of corresponding sides in proportion and the included angles ≅

SSS–Side, Side, Side
3 pairs of corresponding sides in proportion

Tell whether the triangles are similar by SAS~ or by SSS~.

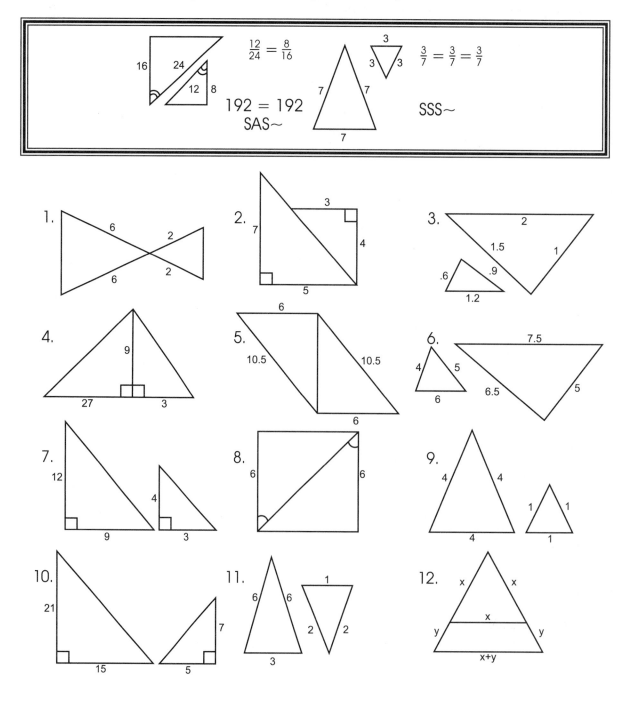

Practice with Similar Triangles

State whether each pair of triangles is similar by AA~, SSS~ or SAS~. If none of these apply, write N.

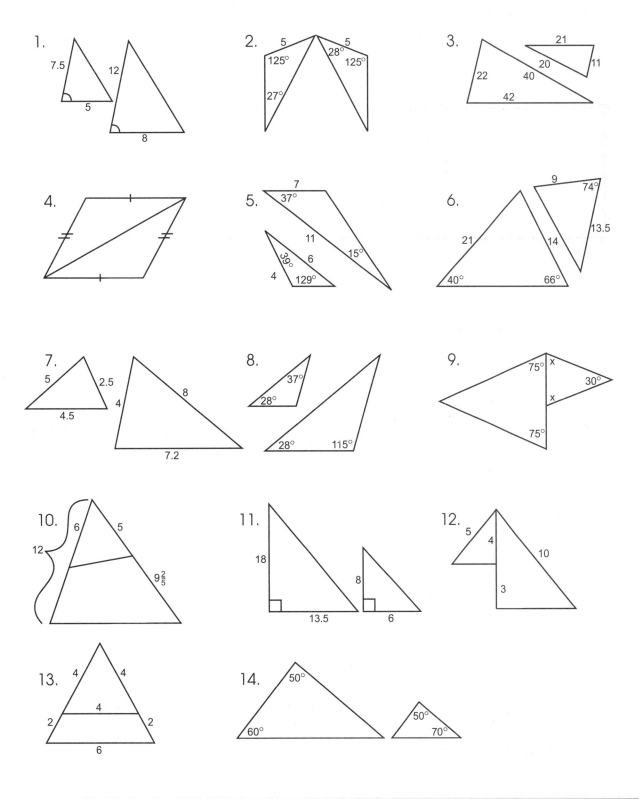

Perimeter and Similar Triangles

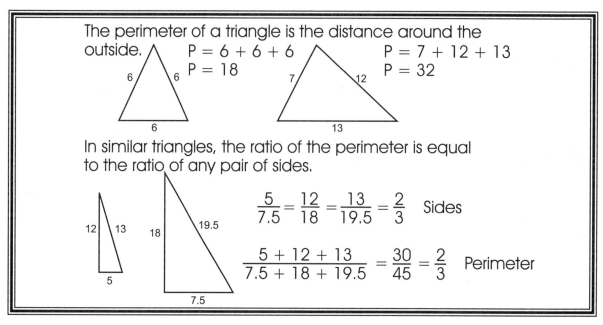

The perimeter of a triangle is the distance around the outside.

$P = 6 + 6 + 6$
$P = 18$

$P = 7 + 12 + 13$
$P = 32$

In similar triangles, the ratio of the perimeter is equal to the ratio of any pair of sides.

$$\frac{5}{7.5} = \frac{12}{18} = \frac{13}{19.5} = \frac{2}{3} \quad \text{Sides}$$

$$\frac{5 + 12 + 13}{7.5 + 18 + 19.5} = \frac{30}{45} = \frac{2}{3} \quad \text{Perimeter}$$

Find the perimeter.

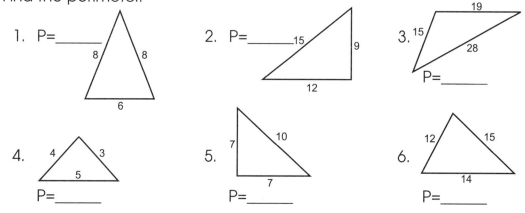

1. P=_____

2. P=_____

3. P=_____

4. P=_____

5. P=_____

6. P=_____

For each pair of similar triangles, find the ratio of the perimeter of the large figure to the perimeter of the smaller.

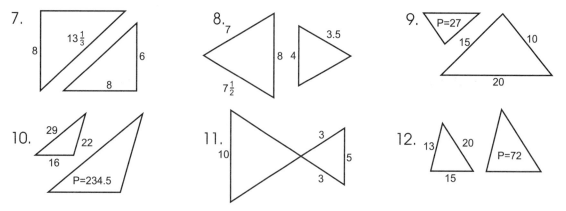

7.

8.

9.   P=27

10.   P=234.5

11.

12.   P=72

Name _____   Date _____

Sierpinski Triangle

A **fractal** is a self-similar object; that is, part of the object looks like the whole object.

Below is the first stage of a fractal called the **Sierpinski Triangle**. It is created by dividing a triangle into four congruent triangles and shading the center triangle.

Stage 2: Connect the midpoints of the sides of each of the three unshaded triangles. Shade the center triangle of each section.
Stage 3: Repeat the steps of Stage 2 for each of the unshaded triangles.
Stage 4: Repeat the steps of Stage 2 for each of the unshaded triangles.

How does the number of unshaded triangles change from step to step?

_____

A Chaotic Triangle

Work with a partner. Use a ruler and a number cube.

1. Mark any point in the triangle. That mark is the starting point.
2. Roll the number cube. For a roll of: 1 or 2, use vertex A
                                                3 or 4, use vertex B
                                                5 or 6, use vertex C
3. Mark the point halfway between the starting point and the vertex from step 2.
4. Repeat step 2. Mark the point halfway between the point marked in step 3 and the vertex determined by rolling the number cube.
5. Repeat the process approximately 100 times: roll the number cube, mark the point halfway between the last marked point and the appropriate vertex.
6. Describe the resulting pattern. _____

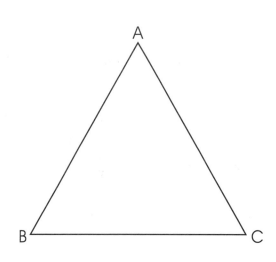

Parallel and Perpendicular Triangles

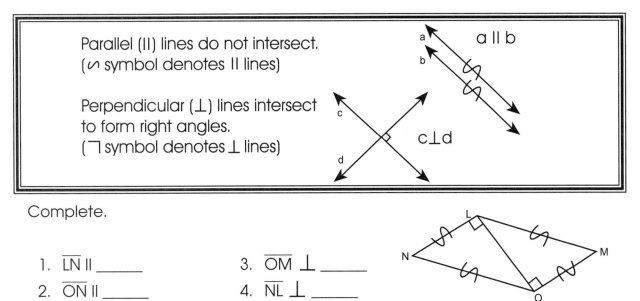

Parallel (‖) lines do not intersect.
(∿ symbol denotes ‖ lines)

Perpendicular (⊥) lines intersect
to form right angles.
(⌐ symbol denotes ⊥ lines)

a ‖ b

c ⊥ d

Complete.

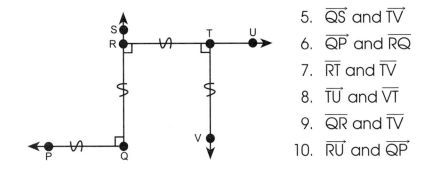

1. $\overleftrightarrow{LN}$ ‖ _____

2. $\overleftrightarrow{ON}$ ‖ _____

3. $\overleftrightarrow{OM}$ ⊥ _____

4. $\overleftrightarrow{NL}$ ⊥ _____

Tell whether each pair of segments or rays is parallel, perpendicular or neither.

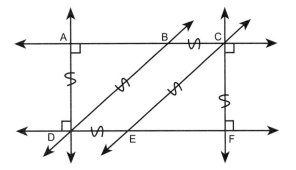

5. $\overleftrightarrow{QS}$ and $\overleftrightarrow{TV}$

6. $\overrightarrow{QP}$ and $\overrightarrow{RQ}$

7. $\overrightarrow{RT}$ and $\overleftrightarrow{TV}$

8. $\overrightarrow{TU}$ and $\overrightarrow{VT}$

9. $\overrightarrow{QR}$ and $\overleftrightarrow{TV}$

10. $\overleftrightarrow{RU}$ and $\overrightarrow{QP}$

11. $\overleftrightarrow{AC}$ and $\overleftrightarrow{DE}$

12. $\overleftrightarrow{CE}$ and $\overleftrightarrow{CF}$

13. $\overleftrightarrow{CF}$ and $\overleftrightarrow{AC}$

14. $\overleftrightarrow{CF}$ and $\overleftrightarrow{AD}$

15. $\overleftrightarrow{DF}$ and $\overleftrightarrow{AD}$

16. $\overleftrightarrow{BD}$ and $\overleftrightarrow{BC}$

17. $\overleftrightarrow{DF}$ and $\overleftrightarrow{EC}$

18. $\overleftrightarrow{BC}$ and $\overleftrightarrow{AD}$

19. $\overleftrightarrow{CE}$ and $\overleftrightarrow{DB}$

20. $\overleftrightarrow{AB}$ and $\overleftrightarrow{EF}$

Angles Formed by Intersecting Lines

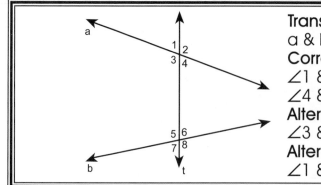

Transversal t intersects lines a & b forming 8 angles.
Corresponding angles:
∠1 & ∠5, ∠3 & ∠7, ∠2 & ∠6, ∠4 & ∠8
Alternate interior angles:
∠3 & ∠6, ∠4 & ∠5
Alternate exterior angles:
∠1 & ∠8, ∠2 & ∠7

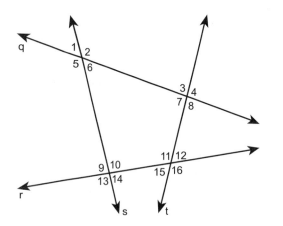

1. Name 2 pairs of alternate interior angles along transversal s; along transversal q.

2. Name 4 pairs of corresponding angles along transversal t;

   along transversal r.

3. Name 2 pairs of alternate exterior angles along transversal q; along transversal t.

For each pair of angles, name the transversal and the kind of angles.

4. ∠11 & ∠8   5. ∠1 & ∠14   6. ∠13 & ∠15

7. ∠4 & ∠5   8. ∠10 & ∠12   9. ∠6 & ∠9

10. ∠2 & ∠4   11. ∠7 & ∠12   12. ∠7 & ∠5

13. ∠16 & ∠9   14. ∠5 & ∠10   15. ∠3 & ∠16

Corresponding Angles Formed by Parallel Lines

When 2 or more parallel lines are cut by a transversal, corresponding angles are congruent.

d ‖ f   m ∠1 = 106°
m ∠2 = 74°

Find the measures of angles 1-22.

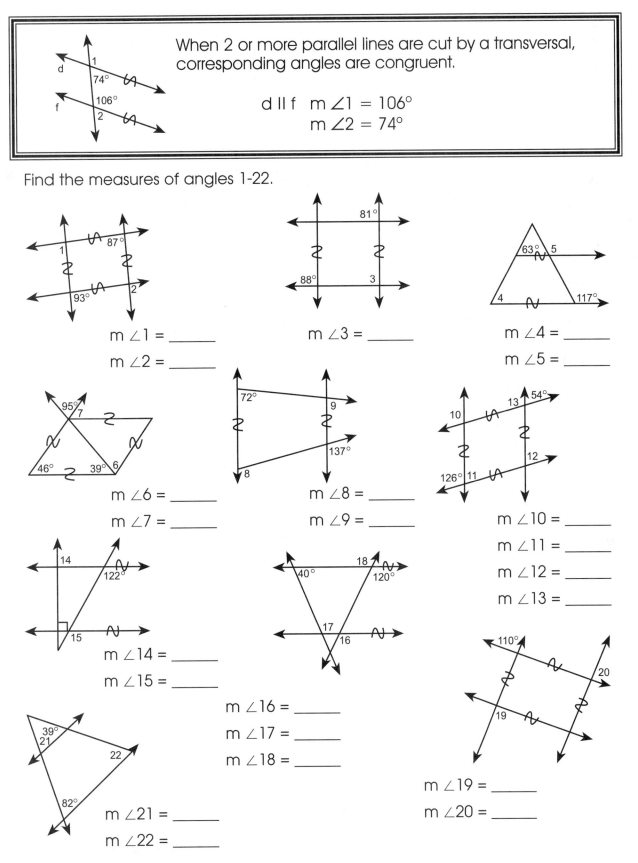

m ∠1 = _____
m ∠2 = _____

m ∠3 = _____

m ∠4 = _____
m ∠5 = _____

m ∠6 = _____
m ∠7 = _____

m ∠8 = _____
m ∠9 = _____

m ∠10 = _____
m ∠11 = _____
m ∠12 = _____
m ∠13 = _____

m ∠14 = _____
m ∠15 = _____

m ∠16 = _____
m ∠17 = _____
m ∠18 = _____

m ∠19 = _____
m ∠20 = _____

m ∠21 = _____
m ∠22 = _____

Name _____   Date _____

Other Angles Formed by Parallel Lines

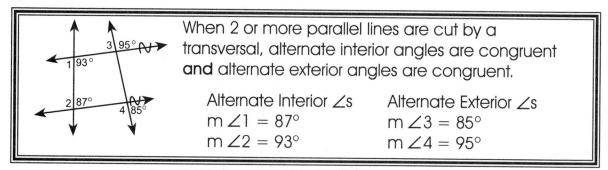

When 2 or more parallel lines are cut by a transversal, alternate interior angles are congruent **and** alternate exterior angles are congruent.

Alternate Interior ∠s	Alternate Exterior ∠s
m ∠1 = 87°	m ∠3 = 85°
m ∠2 = 93°	m ∠4 = 95°

Find the measures of angles 1-25.

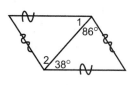

m ∠1 = _____

m ∠2 = _____

m ∠3 = _____

m ∠4 = _____

m ∠5 = _____

m ∠6 = _____

m ∠7 = _____

m ∠8 = _____

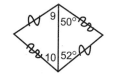

m ∠9 = _____

m ∠10 = _____

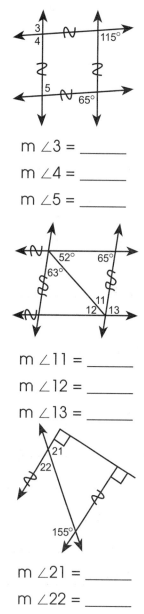

m ∠11 = _____

m ∠12 = _____

m ∠13 = _____

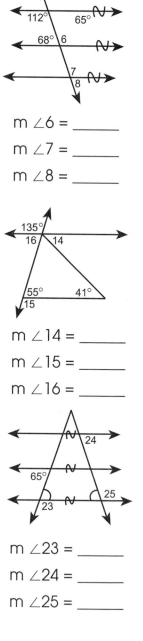

m ∠14 = _____

m ∠15 = _____

m ∠16 = _____

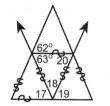

m ∠17 = _____

m ∠18 = _____

m ∠19 = _____

m ∠20 = _____

m ∠21 = _____

m ∠22 = _____

m ∠23 = _____

m ∠24 = _____

m ∠25 = _____

More Parallel Lines

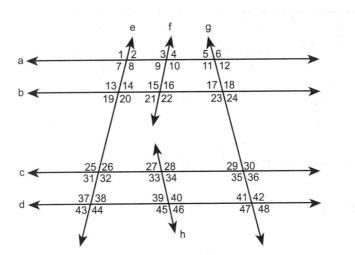

a ∥ b ∥ c ∥ d, e ∥ f, g ∥ h

Fill in the blanks.

1. ∠1 ≅ _____

2. ∠5 ≅ _____

3. If m ∠1 = 100° then m ∠10 = _____

4. If m ∠37 = 105° then m ∠13 = _____

5. If m ∠26 = 80° then m ∠22 = _____

6. If m ∠5 = 70° then m ∠17 = _____

7. If m ∠12 = 65° then m ∠35 = _____

8. If m ∠14 = 85° then m ∠21 = _____

9. If m ∠46 = 73° then m ∠41 = _____

10. If m ∠23 = 132° then m ∠6 = _____

11. If m ∠22 = 120° then m ∠19 = _____

12. If m ∠4 = 55° then m ∠22 = _____

13. If m ∠27 = 80° then m ∠46 = _____

14. If m ∠37 = 104° then m ∠32 = _____

15. If m ∠19 = 76° then m ∠22 = _____

Name _____   Date _____

Can You Rise to the Challenge?

Find the measures of the lettered angles.

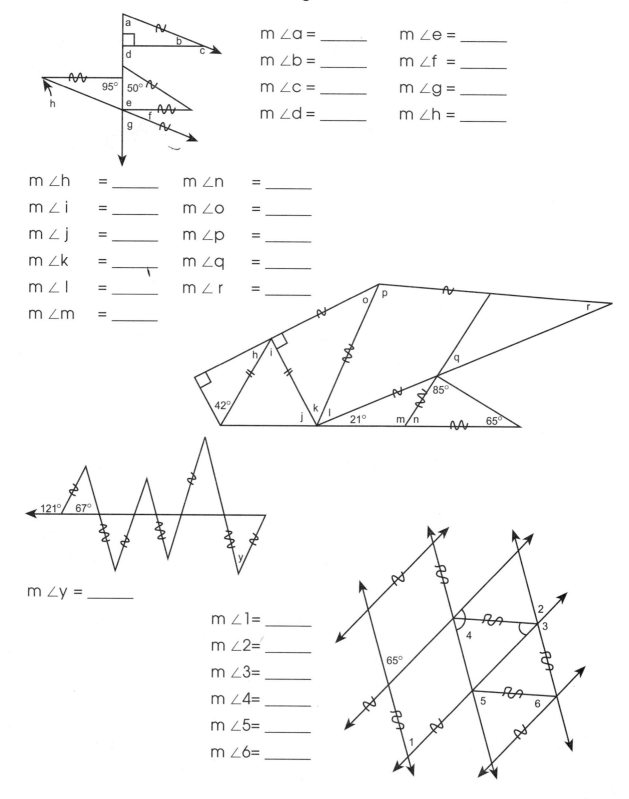

m ∠a = _____   m ∠e = _____

m ∠b = _____   m ∠f = _____

m ∠c = _____   m ∠g = _____

m ∠d = _____   m ∠h = _____

m ∠h   = _____   m ∠n   = _____

m ∠i   = _____   m ∠o   = _____

m ∠j   = _____   m ∠p   = _____

m ∠k   = _____   m ∠q   = _____

m ∠l   = _____   m ∠r   = _____

m ∠m = _____

m ∠y = _____

m ∠1= _____

m ∠2= _____

m ∠3= _____

m ∠4= _____

m ∠5= _____

m ∠6= _____

Line Design

To form a curve from straight lines:

1. Start with an angle

2. Divide the sides into equal parts.

3. Connect the points as shown.

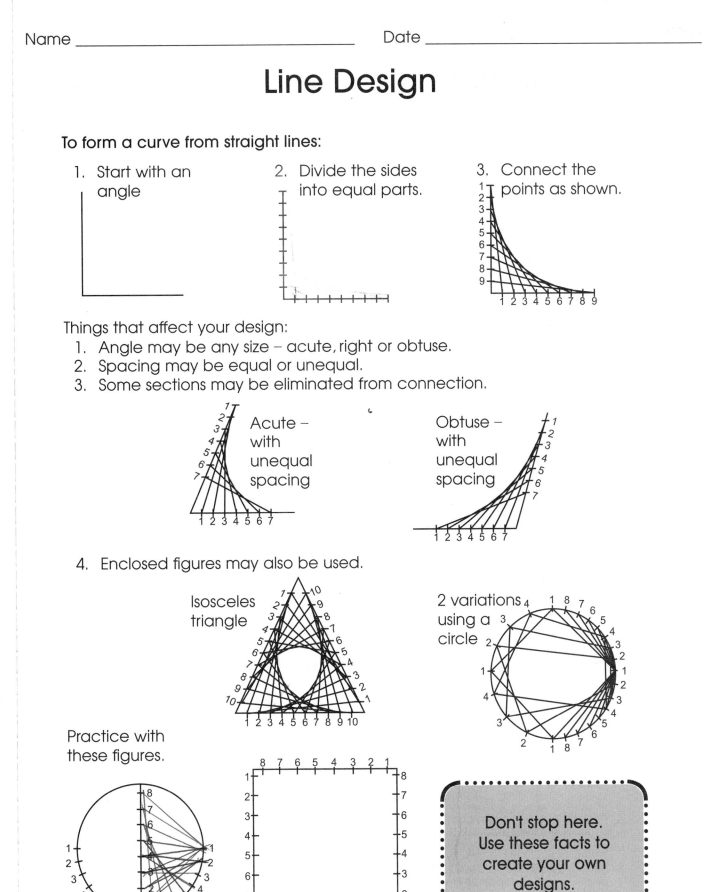

Things that affect your design:
1. Angle may be any size – acute, right or obtuse.
2. Spacing may be equal or unequal.
3. Some sections may be eliminated from connection.

Acute – with unequal spacing

Obtuse – with unequal spacing

4. Enclosed figures may also be used.

Isosceles triangle

2 variations using a circle

Practice with these figures.

Don't stop here. Use these facts to create your own designs.

Parts of Polygons

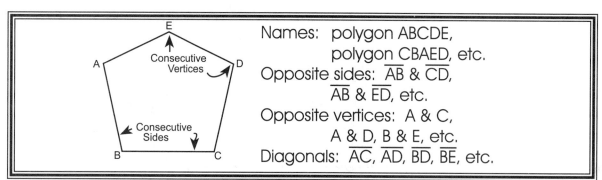

Names: polygon ABCDE,
            polygon CBAED, etc.
Opposite sides: $\overline{AB}$ & $\overline{CD}$,
            $\overline{AB}$ & $\overline{ED}$, etc.
Opposite vertices: A & C,
            A & D, B & E, etc.
Diagonals: $\overline{AC}$, $\overline{AD}$, $\overline{BD}$, $\overline{BE}$, etc.

1. Name the polygon in the example in two different ways, starting with E.

2. Name two sides consecutive to $\overline{AE}$.

3. Name two vertices consecutive to C.

Complete #4-11 with **all** possible answers.

Using figure #1...

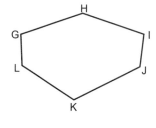

4. Opposite sides $\overline{GH}$.

5. Opposite vertices K.

6. Name all diagonals from I.

Figure #1

Using figure #2...

7. Name this polygon in two different ways, starting with G.

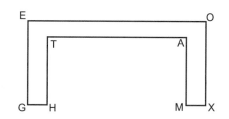

8. Name two sides consecutive to $\overline{GH}$.

9. Name two vertices consecutive to O.

10. List all sides that are opposite $\overline{GH}$.

Figure #2

11. List all vertices that are opposite O.

Name _____   Date _____

Classifying Polygons

Special Names		Other Names	
# of sides	Polygon	# of sides	Polygon
3	triangle	13	13-gon
4	quadrilateral	25	25-gon
5	pentagon	102	102-gon
6	hexagon		
8	octagon	**Regular Polygons:**	
10	decagon	All sides are congruent &	
12	dodecagon	all angles are congruent	

Classify each polygon. Use a special name if possible.

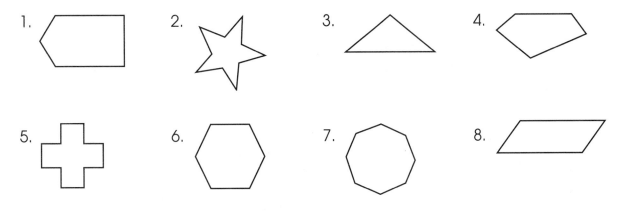

1.   2.   3.   4.

5.   6.   7.   8.

The polygons shown are regular polygons.

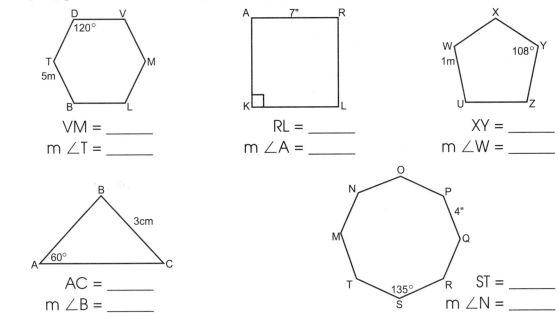

VM = _____
m ∠T = _____

RL = _____
m ∠A = _____

XY = _____
m ∠W = _____

AC = _____
m ∠B = _____

ST = _____
m ∠N = _____

Angle Measures in Convex Polygons

In a convex polygon, all angles open inward.
To find the sum of the
measures of the angles
in a convex polygon:
1. Draw all diagonals
   from one vertex
2. Multiply the number of   Sum of angles
   triangles formed by 180°.   3 • 180 = 540°

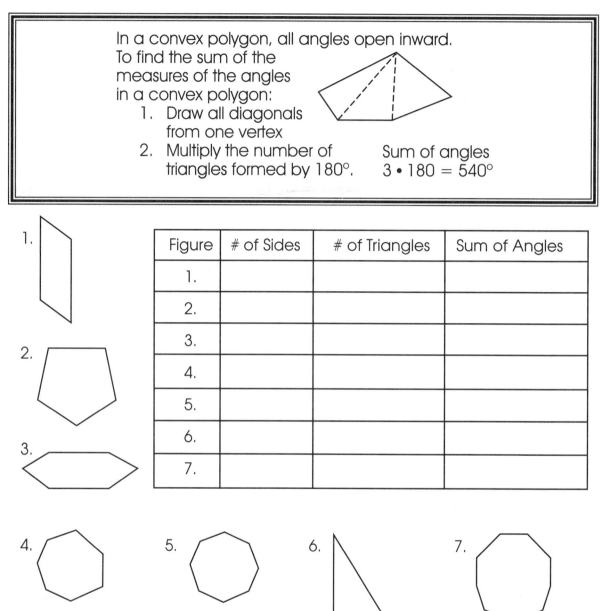

Figure	# of Sides	# of Triangles	Sum of Angles
1.			
2.			
3.			
4.			
5.			
6.			
7.			

8. Based on the chart results how many triangles would be formed in an n-gon?

9. What is the sum of the measures of the angles in a convex n-gon?

10. Find the sum of the measures of the angles in a convex 21-gon.

Name _____   Date _____

Angle Measures in Regular Polygons

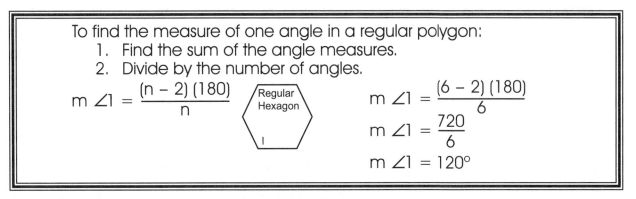

To find the measure of one angle in a regular polygon:
1. Find the sum of the angle measures.
2. Divide by the number of angles.

$$m \angle 1 = \frac{(n-2)(180)}{n}$$

Regular Hexagon

$$m \angle 1 = \frac{(6-2)(180)}{6}$$

$$m \angle 1 = \frac{720}{6}$$

$$m \angle 1 = 120°$$

Find the measure of one angle of these polygons.

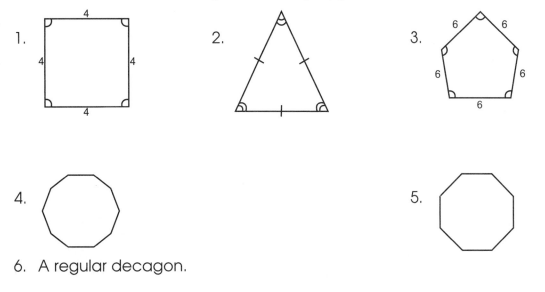

1.

2.

3.

4.

5.

6. A regular decagon.

7. A regular dodecagon.

8. A regular 20-gon.

9. A regular 100-gon.

10. A regular n-gon.

Parallelograms

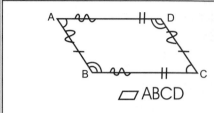

Opposite sides are parallel.
Opposite sides are congruent.
Opposite angles are congruent.
Consecutive angles are supplementary.

◻ ABCD

Find the indicated measures.

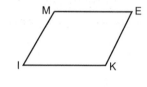

1. MI = 8; KE = _____

2. ME = 11; IK = _____

3. M ∠I = 47°; m ∠E = _____; m ∠K = _____

4. $\overline{ME} \cong$ _____

5. ∠M ≅ _____

6. m ∠M + _____ = 180°

7. $\overline{KE} \cong$ _____

8. ∠I ≅ _____

9. m ∠M = 120°; m ∠E = _____; m ∠I = _____

10. m ∠K + _____ = 180°

11. m ∠M + m ∠I + m ∠K + m ∠E = _____

A diagonal of a ◻ divides it into 2 ≅ triangles.
The diagonals of a ◻ bisect each other.
(Note: Bisect means to cut in half.)

◻ PAUL

12. ΔQRT ≅ _____

13. ΔTQS ≅ _____

14. If m ∠1 + m ∠2 = 80°; m ∠QRS = _____

15. TU = 5, RU = _____

16. QU + US = 14; QU = _____

17. Point U is the midpoint of _____.

18. ΔQUR ≅ _____

19. QS = 7, QU = _____

20. ∠3 ≅ _____

◻ TQRS

Name _____   Date _____

Rectangles, Rhombuses, and Squares

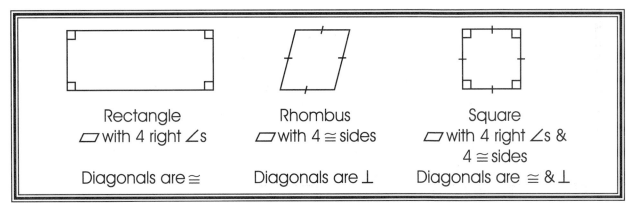

Rectangle	Rhombus	Square
▱ with 4 right ∠s	▱ with 4 ≅ sides	▱ with 4 right ∠s & 4 ≅ sides
Diagonals are ≅	Diagonals are ⊥	Diagonals are ≅ & ⊥

True or False.

1. A rhombus is a parallelogram with four congruent sides.

2. A rectangle is a parallelogram with four right angles.

3. A square is a rectangle and a rhombus.

4. A rhombus is always a square.

5. Every parallelogram is a regular quadrilateral.

6. In a rectangle, the diagonals are perpendicular.

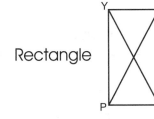

Rectangle

7. Which angles are congruent to ∠PAT?

8. Which segment is congruent to $\overline{YT}$?

9. Which segment is congruent to $\overline{PT}$?

10. Which segments are congruent to $\overline{SD}$?

11. Which segment is congruent to $\overline{MO}$?

12. What is the measure of ∠BOD?

Rhombus

13. Which segments are congruent to $\overline{TV}$?

14. Which angles are congruent to ∠TIM?

15. Which segment is congruent to $\overline{TM}$?

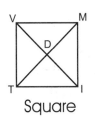

Square

Trapezoids

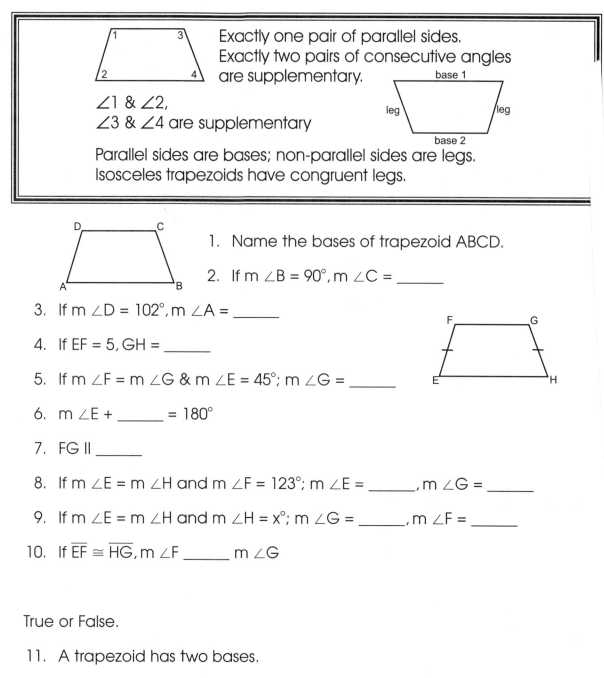

Exactly one pair of parallel sides.
Exactly two pairs of consecutive angles are supplementary.

∠1 & ∠2,
∠3 & ∠4 are supplementary

Parallel sides are bases; non-parallel sides are legs.
Isosceles trapezoids have congruent legs.

1. Name the bases of trapezoid ABCD.

2. If m ∠B = 90°, m ∠C = _____

3. If m ∠D = 102°, m ∠A = _____

4. If EF = 5, GH = _____

5. If m ∠F = m ∠G & m ∠E = 45°; m ∠G = _____

6. m ∠E + _____ = 180°

7. FG || _____

8. If m ∠E = m ∠H and m ∠F = 123°; m ∠E = _____, m ∠G = _____

9. If m ∠E = m ∠H and m ∠H = x°; m ∠G = _____, m ∠F = _____

10. If $\overline{EF} \cong \overline{HG}$, m ∠F _____ m ∠G

True or False.

11. A trapezoid has two bases.

12. A trapezoid may have a right angle.

13. There exists a trapezoid with three congruent sides.

14. The bases of an isosceles trapezoid are congruent.

15. The parallel sides of a trapezoid are called the legs.

Name _____ Date _____

Mixed Practice with Quadrilaterals

a. quadrilateral

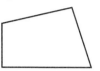

b. square

c. rectangle

d. rhombus

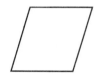

e. parallelogram

f. trapezoid

Write the letter(s) of the correct answer(s).

1. The diagonals are perpendicular.

2. All four angles are congruent.

3. Opposite sides are parallel and congruent.

4. Consecutive angles are supplementary.

5. The diagonals bisect each other.

6. A diagonal forms two non-congruent triangles.

7. Exactly one pair of sides are parallel.

8. Opposite angles have equal measures.

9. The diagonals are congruent.

10. Only two pairs of consecutive angles are supplementary.

11. The measure of each angle is ninety degrees.

12. All four sides are congruent.

Name _____   Date _____

Midpoint Segments

In trapezoid PARK, T is the midpoint of $\overline{PA}$ and D is the midpoint of $\overline{RK}$. $\overline{TD}$ is the **median** of the trapezoid.

$\overline{TD} \parallel \overline{AR}$ and $\overline{TD} \parallel \overline{PK}$; $TD = \dfrac{AR + PK}{2}$

Find answer and cross off in letter bank. Remaining letters spell solution to riddle.

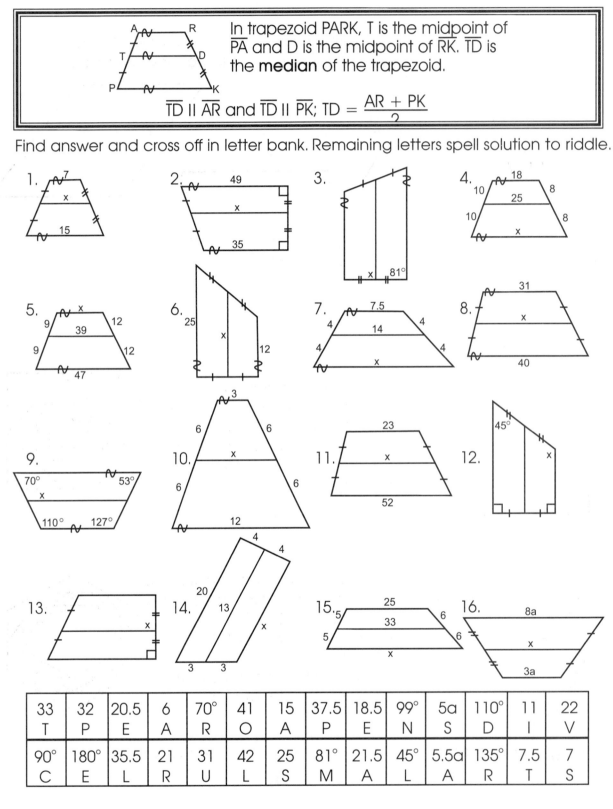

33	32	20.5	6	70°	41	15	37.5	18.5	99°	5a	110°	11	22
T	P	E	A	R	O	A	P	E	N	S	D	I	V
90°	180°	35.5	21	31	42	25	81°	21.5	45°	5.5a	135°	7.5	7
C	E	L	R	U	L	S	M	A	L	A	R	T	S

Segment AP and segment KR are parts of line AP and line KR, which are

___ ___ ___ ___ ___ ___ ___ ___ ___ ___ ___ ___ ___ intersecting parallel lines.

Properties of Midpoints

For each quadrilateral: • Measure to find the midpoints of each side.
                         • Connect the midpoints of consecutive sides.

What kind of quadrilateral is formed?

A logarithmic spiral

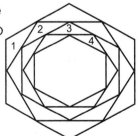

• Locate the midpoint of each side and join consecutive midpoints to form a smaller square.
• Repeat this process at least 12 times.
• Shade the regions as indicated, continuing to the center.

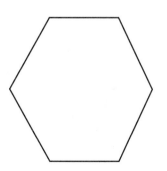

• Locate the midpoint of each side and join consecutive midpoints to form a smaller hexagon.
• Repeat this process at least 12 times.
• Shade the regions as indicated, continuing to the center.

A logarithmic spiral can be made with any regular polygon.

Ordered Pairs and Graphing

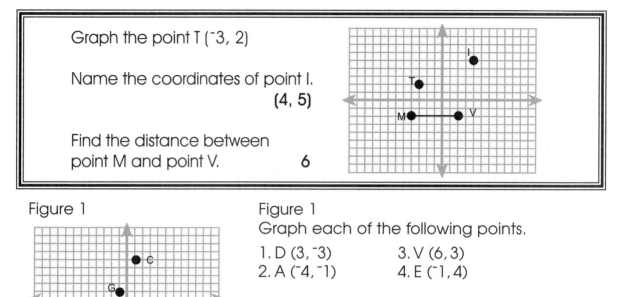

Graph the point T (⁻3, 2)

Name the coordinates of point I.
(4, 5)

Find the distance between
point M and point V.   6

Figure 1

Figure 1
Graph each of the following points.
1. D (3, ⁻3)   3. V (6, 3)
2. A (⁻4, ⁻1)   4. E (⁻1, 4)

Name the coordinates of each point.
5. B   6. C   7. F   8. G

Figure 2
9.   Give the equation for line p; line r.

10. Name the point of intersection of lines
     m and p.

11. Name the coordinates of points A, B and C.
     Find AB and BC.

Figure 2
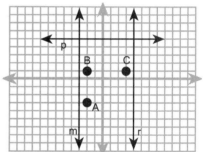

Figure 3
12. Name two points that are 3 units apart.

13. Name two points that are 5 units from K.

14. Find BF.

15. Find FV.

16. Give the equation for $\overleftrightarrow{TB}$.

Figure 3
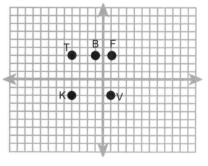

Name _____   Date _____

The Distance Formula

The distance between
2 points: $(x_1, y_1), (x_2, y_2)$

$$D = \sqrt{(x_2 - x_1)^2 + (y_2 - y_1)^2}$$

Find the distance
between $(^-3, 2)$ and $(1, ^-2)$
$$D = \sqrt{(1 - ^-3)^2 + (^-2 - 2)^2}$$
$$= \sqrt{(4)^2 + (^-4)^2} = \sqrt{16 + 16}$$
$$= \sqrt{32} = \sqrt{2 \cdot 2 \cdot 2 \cdot 2 \cdot 2}$$
$$= 4\sqrt{2}$$

Find the distance between these pairs of points.

1. $(6, 4)$ and $(2, 1)$

2. $(^-2, ^-4)$ and $(3, 8)$

3. $(0, 0)$ and $(5, 10)$

4. $(^-5, 2)$ and $(7, ^-7)$

5. $(0, ^-8)$ and $(8, 7)$

6. $(^-2, 11)$ and $(4, 3)$

7. $(2, 1)$ and $(4, 0)$

8. $(6, 4)$ and $(6, ^-2)$

9. $(^-2, 2)$ and $(4, ^-1)$

10. $(^-3, ^-5)$ and $(2, 5)$

11. $(^-4, 0)$ and $(2, 3)$

12. $(^-1, 5)$ and $(3, ^-3)$

13. $(0, 0)$ and $(3, 4)$

14. $(1, 8)$ and $(3, 10)$

15. $(9, 8)$ and $(^-3, 4)$

16. $(2, 2)$ and $(2, 4)$

The Midpoint Formula

To find the coordinates of the midpoint of a segment with endpoints $E_1(x_1 , y_1)$ and $E_2(x_2 , y_2)$:

$$x_m = \frac{x_1 + x_2}{2} \qquad y_m = \frac{y_1 + y_2}{2}$$

To find the midpoint of the segment with these endpoints $E_1(^-6, 1)$ and $E_2(3, 7)$:

$$x_m = \frac{^-6 + 3}{2} \qquad y_m = \frac{1 + 7}{2}$$

$$= -\frac{3}{2} \qquad\qquad = 4$$

$$M\left(-\frac{3}{2}, 4\right)$$

Find the midpoint of the segments with these endpoints.

1. $(1, 8)$ and $(3, 10)$

2. $(2, 2)$ and $(2, 4)$

3. $(2, 3)$ and $(^-1, ^-5)$

4. $(9, 8)$ and $(^-3, 4)$

5. $(^1/_2, 1)$ and $(4^1/_2, ^-7)$

6. $(0.6, ^-1.2)$ and $(^-0.6, 1.2)$

7. $(^-2, 2)$ and $(4, ^-1)$

8. $(^-3, ^-5)$ and $(2, 5)$

9. $(^-4, 0)$ and $(2, 3)$

10. $(^-1, 5)$ and $(3, ^-3)$

11. $(0, 0)$ and $(3, 4)$

12. $(6, 4)$ and $(2, 1)$

Given the midpoint and one endpoint of a segment, find the other endpoint.

13. $E_1 (5, ^-1)$ and $M (^-3, 7)$

14. $E_1 (2, 5)$ and $M (^-1, 6)$

15. $E_1 (4, 4)$ and $M (3, 5)$

16. $E_1 (7, 4)$ and $M (3, ^-2)$

Name _____   Date _____

The Slope of a Line

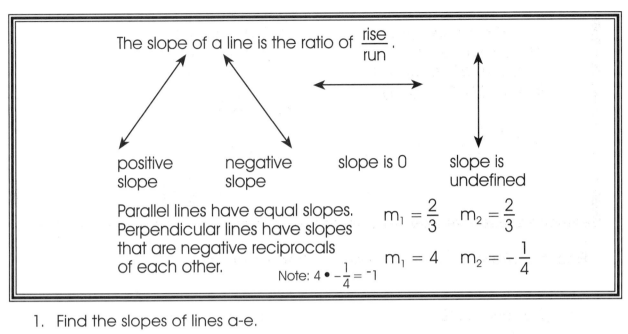

The slope of a line is the ratio of $\frac{rise}{run}$.

positive slope   negative slope   slope is 0   slope is undefined

Parallel lines have equal slopes. Perpendicular lines have slopes that are negative reciprocals of each other.

$m_1 = \frac{2}{3}$ $m_2 = \frac{2}{3}$

$m_1 = 4$ $m_2 = -\frac{1}{4}$

Note: $4 \bullet -\frac{1}{4} = {}^{-}1$

1. Find the slopes of lines a-e.

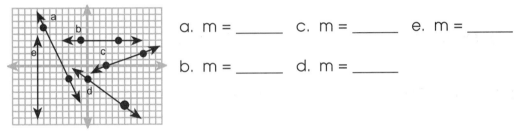

a. m = _____   c. m = _____   e. m = _____

b. m = _____   d. m = _____

2. Tell whether the slopes of lines f-n are positive, negative, 0 or undefined.

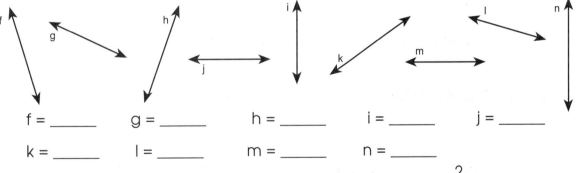

f = _____   g = _____   h = _____   i = _____   j = _____

k = _____   l = _____   m = _____   n = _____

3. Find the slope of a line parallel to a line with slope of 2; $-\frac{2}{9}$

4. Find the slope of a line perpendicular to a line with slope of 2; $-\frac{2}{9}$

Determine if the lines having the following slopes are parallel, perpendicular or neither.

5. $m_1 = 1\frac{1}{2}$ and $m_2 = -\frac{2}{3}$

6. $m_1 = \frac{5}{7}$ and $m_2 = 1\frac{2}{5}$

7. $m_1 = 1\frac{3}{7}$ and $m_2 = \frac{10}{7}$

8. $m_1 = {}^{-}3\frac{2}{3}$ and $m_2 = -\frac{11}{3}$

Polygons with Parallel and Perpendicular Lines

> Parallel lines have slopes that are equal.
> Perpendicular lines have slopes that are negative
> reciprocals of each other.

Determine which sides of quadrilateral QRST are parallel or perpendicular.

Q (0, 0)   R (4, 2)   S (2, 3)   T (0, 2)

slope of $\overline{QR} = \dfrac{2-0}{4-0} = \dfrac{1}{2}$ slope of $\overline{ST} = \dfrac{2-3}{0-2} = \dfrac{1}{2}$

slope of $\overline{RS} = \dfrac{3-2}{2-4} = \dfrac{1}{^-2}$ slope of $\overline{QT} = \dfrac{2-0}{0-0} =$ undefined

$$\overline{QR} \parallel \overline{ST}$$

1. Q (0,0)   R (6, ⁻2)   S (7, 1)   T (1, 3)

2. Q (⁻3, ⁻1)   R (3, 1)   S (1, 3)   T (⁻2, 2)

3. Q (1, ⁻3)   R (⁻2, 0)   S (7, ⁻1)   T (4, 2)

4. Q (2, ⁻2)   R (5, 0)   S (1, 4)   T (⁻5, 0)

Determine if $\triangle ABC$ is a right triangle. Then, classify it as scalene, isosceles or equilateral. (Hint: Use slope and distance formulas.)

5. A (⁻2, 3)   B (1, 5)   C (3, 2)

6. A (0, 0)   B (3, ⁻1)   C (1, 2)

7. A (⁻3, 0)   B (0, ⁻4)   C (0, 0)

8. A (1, 1)   B (1, 5)   C (3, 3)

Equation of a Line in Standard Form: Ax + By = C

I.   Given the slope and a point.

$$m = \frac{1}{4}, (^-4, 3)$$

Use slope-intercept form and solve for b.

$y = mx + b$ $y = \frac{1}{4}x + 4$

$3 = \frac{1}{4}(^-4) + b$ $4y = x + 16$

$3 = ^-1 + b$ $-x + 4y = 16$

$4 = b$

Find the equations of the lines with the following conditions. Write the equations in standard form.

1. $m = ^-3 \ (1, 3)$ 2. $m = \frac{2}{3} \ (3, ^-2)$ 3. $m = \frac{1}{2} \ (2, ^-1)$

4. $m = -\frac{1}{2} \ (\frac{1}{2}, 1)$ 5. $m = 3 \ (^-1, ^-7)$ 6. $m = \frac{5}{7} \ (1, ^-1)$

7. $m = ^-1 \ (3, 4)$ 8. $m = 1 \ (5, 2)$ 9. $m = \frac{2}{5} \ (-\frac{1}{2}, 1)$

II.   Given two points.

$$(2, 4), (^-1, ^-2)$$
$$m = \frac{y2 - y1}{x2 - x1} = \frac{^-2 - 4}{^-1 - 2} = \frac{^-6}{^-3} = 2$$

$y = 2x + b$ $y = 2x + 0$

$4 = 2(2) + b$ $y = 2x$

$4 = 4 + b$ $2x - y = 0$

$0 = b$

Find the equations of the lines with the following conditions. Write the equations in standard form.

1. $(^-1, 9), (2, 0)$ 2. $(3, ^-2), (^-3, ^-6)$ 3. $(4, 0), (6, 1)$

4. $(2, \frac{1}{4}) \ (\frac{1}{2}, 1)$ 5. $(1, ^-1), (2, 2)$ 6. $(1, ^-1), (8, 4)$

7. $(2, 5), (^-3, 10)$ 8. $(6, 3), (^-1, ^-4)$ 9. $(^-3, 0), (2, 2)$

Equation of a Line in Standard Form: Ax + By = C

II.   Given a parallel line.

> Parallel to y = 2x − 1 through (2, 2).
> Remember, parallel lines have the same slope.
> m = 2 (2, 2)
>
> y = 2x + b   y = 2x − 2
> 2 = 2 (2) + b   ⁻2x + y = ⁻2
> 2 = 4 + b   2x − y = 2
> ⁻2 = b

Find the equations of the lines with the following conditions. Write the equations in standard form.

1. Parallel to 3x + 4y = 7 through (1, 3)
2. Parallel to 2x − 3y = 8 through (2, 2)
3. Parallel to x + y = 9 through (⁻1, 6)
4. Parallel to x − 2y = 4 through (4, 4)
5. Parallel to 3x − 7y = 9 through (3, ⁻2)

IV.   Given a perpendicular line.

> Perpendicular to y = 2x − 1 through (2, 2).
> Remember, perpendicular lines have slopes that are negative reciprocals of each other.
>
> $m = \dfrac{^-1}{2}$ (because $\dfrac{^-1}{2} \cdot 2 = -1$)   (2, 2)
>
> $y = \dfrac{^-1}{2}x + b$ $y = -\dfrac{1}{2}x + 3$
>
> $2 = \dfrac{^-1}{2}(2) + b$ x + 2y = 6
>
> 3 = b

Find the equations of the lines with the following conditions. Write the equations in standard form.

1. Perpendicular to 3x + 4y = 7 through (1, 3).
2. Perpendicular to 2x + 3y = 8 through (2, 2).
3. Perpendicular to x + y = 9 through (⁻1, 6).

Graphing Lines

I.   Plotting points.

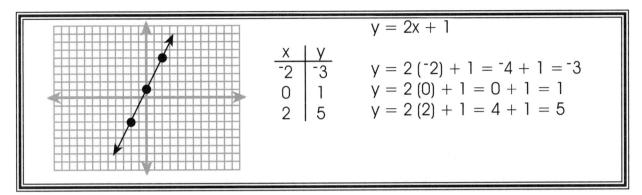

Graph the following lines by plotting points. Use your own graph paper.

1. $y = x + 3$

2. $y = -x + 4$

3. $y = \frac{1}{2}x + 2$

4. $y = -\frac{1}{3}x + 1$

5. $y = 2x - 3$

6. $y = \frac{1}{2}x - 3$

7. $2x - 3y = 6$

8. $3x + 4y = 12$

9. $5x - 2y = 10$

II.   Slope-Intercept.

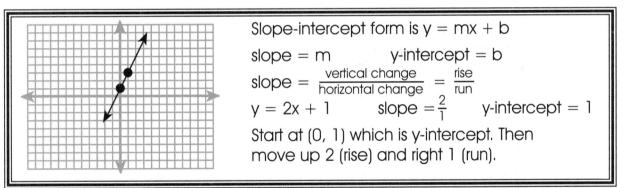

Graph the following lines by using the slope and y-intercept. Use your own graph paper.

1. $y = x + 3$

2. $y = -x + 4$

3. $y = \frac{1}{2}x + 2$

4. $y = \frac{-1}{3}x + 1$

5. $y = 2x - 3$

6. $y = \frac{1}{2}x - 3$

7. $2x - 3y = 6$

8. $3x + 4y = 12$

9. $5x - 2y = 10$

Solving Systems of Equations

I. Graphing.

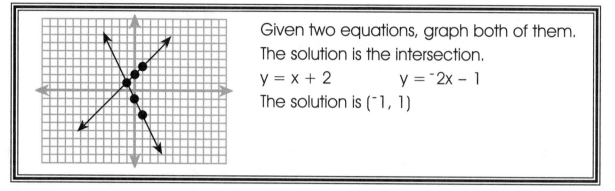

Given two equations, graph both of them.
The solution is the intersection.

$y = x + 2$ $y = ^-2x - 1$

The solution is $(^-1, 1)$

Solve the following systems of equations by graphing.

1. $y = x + 1$
   $y = 3x - 3$

2. $y = 2x$
   $y = x - 1$

3. $y = 5x$
   $y = -\dfrac{1}{2}x$

4. $y = 3x + 14$
   $y = ^-2x - 6$

5. $3x + 2y = 7$
   $x + 2y = 1$

6. $2x + 5y = 27$
   $2x - 3y = ^-13$

7. $3x + y = 9$
   $2x - y = 6$

8. $x + y = ^-7$
   $x - y = 1$

II. Substitution.

Given two equations, substitute one into the other.

$y = x + 2$ $2x + y = ^-1$

$2x + (x + 2) = ^-1$ $y = ^-1 + 2$

$2x + x + 2 = ^-1$ $y = 1$

$3x + 2 = ^-1$ The solution is $(^-1, 1)$

$3x = ^-3$

$x = ^-1$

Solve the following systems of equations using substitution.

1. $y = x + 1$
   $y = 3x - 3$

2. $y = 2x$
   $y = x - 1$

3. $y = 5x$
   $y = -\dfrac{1}{2}x$

4. $y = 3x + 14$
   $y = ^-2x - 6$

5. $3x + 2y = 7$
   $x + 2y = 1$

6. $2x + 5y = 27$
   $2x - 3y = ^-13$

7. $3x + y = 9$
   $2x - y = 6$

8. $x + y = ^-7$
   $x - y = 1$

Solving Systems of Equations

III. Addition.
Given two equations, add a multiple of one to the other so that only one variable remains.

$$y = x + 2 \rightarrow 2y = 2x + 4 \qquad\qquad y = {}^-2x - 1$$

$$\begin{aligned} 2y &= 2x + 4 \\ + y &= {}^-2x - 1 \\ \hline 3y &= 3 \\ y &= 2 \end{aligned} \qquad\qquad \begin{aligned} 1 &= {}^-2x - 1 \\ 2 &= {}^-2x \\ {}^-1 &= x \end{aligned}$$

The solution is $({}^-1, 1)$

Solve the following systems of equations by addition.

1. $y = x + 1$
   $y = 3x - 3$

2. $y = 2x$
   $y = x - 1$

3. $y = 5x$
   $y = -\dfrac{1}{2}x$

4. $y = 3x + 14$
   $y = {}^-2x - 6$

5. $3x + 2y = 7$
   $x + 2y = 1$

6. $2x + 5y = 27$
   $2x - 3y = {}^-13$

7. $3x + y = 9$
   $2x - y = 6$

8. $x + y = {}^-7$
   $x - y = 1$

IV. Matrix.
Given two equations, put the coefficients in a matrix to solve for x and y.

$$ax + by = c \qquad\qquad 2x + 1y = {}^-1$$
$$dx + ey = f \qquad\qquad {}^-1x + 1y = 2$$

$$x = \frac{\begin{vmatrix} c & b \\ f & e \end{vmatrix}}{\begin{vmatrix} a & b \\ d & e \end{vmatrix}} = \frac{ce - bf}{ae - bd} \qquad x = \frac{\begin{vmatrix} {}^-1 & 1 \\ 2 & 1 \end{vmatrix}}{\begin{vmatrix} 2 & 1 \\ {}^-1 & 1 \end{vmatrix}} = \frac{({}^-1)(1) - (2)(1)}{(2)(1) - ({}^-1)(1)} = \frac{{}^-1 - 2}{2 - {}^-1} = \frac{{}^-3}{3} = {}^-1$$

$$y = \frac{\begin{vmatrix} a & c \\ d & f \end{vmatrix}}{\begin{vmatrix} a & b \\ d & e \end{vmatrix}} = \frac{af - cd}{ae - bd} \qquad y = \frac{\begin{vmatrix} 2 & {}^-1 \\ {}^-1 & 2 \end{vmatrix}}{\begin{vmatrix} 2 & 1 \\ {}^-1 & 1 \end{vmatrix}} = \frac{(2)(2) - ({}^-1)({}^-1)}{(2)(1) - ({}^-1)(1)} = \frac{4 - 1}{2 - {}^-1} = \frac{3}{3} = 1$$

The solution is $({}^-1, 1)$

Solve the following systems of equations using a matrix.

1. $y = x + 1$
   $y = 3x - 3$

2. $y = 2x$
   $y = x - 1$

3. $y = 5x$
   $y = -\dfrac{1}{2}x$

4. $y = 3x + 14$
   $y = {}^-2x - 6$

5. $3x + 2y = 7$

6. $2x + 5y = 27$

7. $3x + y = 9$

8. $x + y = {}^-7$

More Fun

Find one of the four figures (A, B, C and D) in each of the boxes below.
The four figures can be rotated in any way.

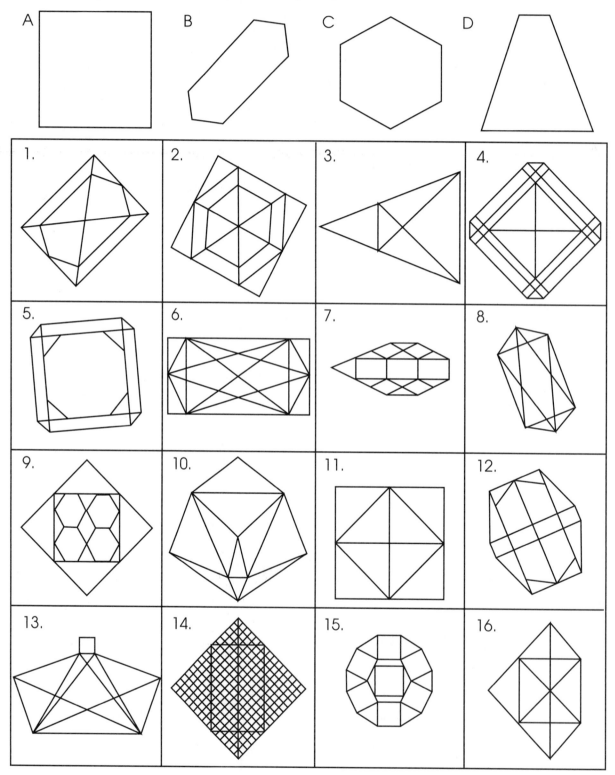

Name _____ Date _____

Parts of a Circle

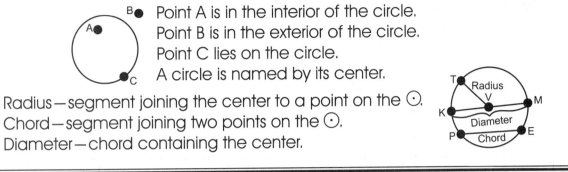

Point A is in the interior of the circle.
Point B is in the exterior of the circle.
Point C lies on the circle.
A circle is named by its center.

Radius — segment joining the center to a point on the ⊙.
Chord — segment joining two points on the ⊙.
Diameter — chord containing the center.

Identify each segment as a radius, chord or diameter.

1. $\overline{OA}$ 3. $\overline{LW}$ 5. $\overline{DW}$ 7. $\overline{AW}$

2. $\overline{DL}$ 4. $\overline{WO}$ 6. $\overline{LA}$ 8. $\overline{OL}$

Name all examples of each term shown.

Figure 1

9. Radius

10. Chord

11. Center

12. Diameter

Figure 1

Figure 2

13. Name all the points in the interior of the circle.

14. Name all the points in the exterior of the circle.

15. Name all the points on the circle.

16. Name the center of the circle.

17. Name all segments that are a radius of the circle.

18. Name all segments that are a diameter of the circle.

19. Name all segments that are neither a radius nor a diameter of the circle.

20. Name all segments that are chords of the circle.

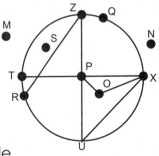

Figure 2

Secants and Tangents

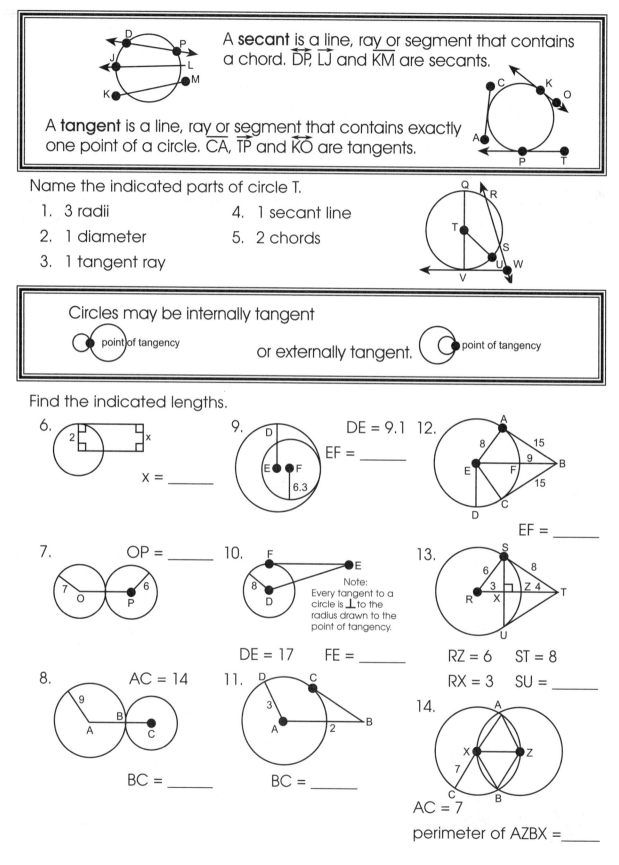

A **secant** is a line, ray or segment that contains a chord. $\overleftrightarrow{DP}$, $\overrightarrow{LJ}$ and $\overline{KM}$ are secants.

A **tangent** is a line, ray or segment that contains exactly one point of a circle. $\overline{CA}$, $\overrightarrow{TP}$ and $\overleftrightarrow{KO}$ are tangents.

Name the indicated parts of circle T.

1. 3 radii
2. 1 diameter
3. 1 tangent ray
4. 1 secant line
5. 2 chords

Circles may be internally tangent point of tangency or externally tangent. point of tangency

Find the indicated lengths.

6. 2   x

X = _____

7.   OP = _____
   7   O   P   6

8.   AC = 14
   9   B   A   C

BC = _____

9.   D   DE = 9.1
   E   F   EF = _____
   6.3

10.   F   E
   8   D
   Note: Every tangent to a circle is ⊥ to the radius drawn to the point of tangency.
   DE = 17   FE = _____

11.   D   C
   3   A   B   2
   BC = _____

12.   A
   8   15
   E   9   F   B
   15   C
   D
   EF = _____

13.   S
   6   8
   R   3   Z 4   T
   X   U
   RZ = 6   ST = 8
   RX = 3   SU = _____

14.   A
   X   Z
   7   B
   C
   AC = 7
   perimeter of AZBX = _____

Published by Instructional Fair. Copyright protected.   Page 76   0-7424-1777-8 *Intro to Geometry*

Arcs and Angles

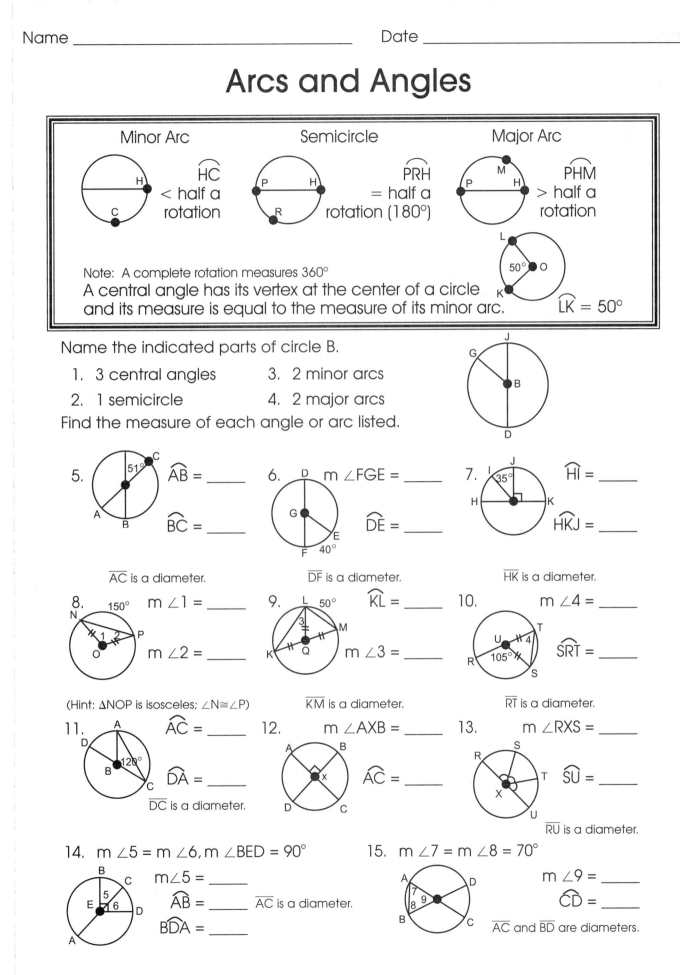

Minor Arc   Semicircle   Major Arc

$\overset{\frown}{HC}$ < half a rotation

$\overset{\frown}{PRH}$ = half a rotation (180°)

$\overset{\frown}{PHM}$ > half a rotation

Note: A complete rotation measures 360°
A central angle has its vertex at the center of a circle and its measure is equal to the measure of its minor arc.

$\overset{\frown}{LK} = 50°$

Name the indicated parts of circle B.

1. 3 central angles   3. 2 minor arcs
2. 1 semicircle   4. 2 major arcs

Find the measure of each angle or arc listed.

5. $\overset{\frown}{AB}$ = _____

$\overset{\frown}{BC}$ = _____

$\overline{AC}$ is a diameter.

6. m ∠FGE = _____

$\overset{\frown}{DE}$ = _____

$\overline{DF}$ is a diameter.

7. $\overset{\frown}{HI}$ = _____

$\overset{\frown}{HKJ}$ = _____

$\overline{HK}$ is a diameter.

8. m ∠1 = _____

m ∠2 = _____

(Hint: △NOP is isosceles; ∠N≅∠P)

9. $\overset{\frown}{KL}$ = _____

m ∠3 = _____

$\overline{KM}$ is a diameter.

10. m ∠4 = _____

$\overset{\frown}{SRT}$ = _____

$\overline{RT}$ is a diameter.

11. $\overset{\frown}{AC}$ = _____

$\overset{\frown}{DA}$ = _____

$\overline{DC}$ is a diameter.

12. m ∠AXB = _____

$\overset{\frown}{AC}$ = _____

13. m ∠RXS = _____

$\overset{\frown}{SU}$ = _____

$\overline{RU}$ is a diameter.

14. m ∠5 = m ∠6, m ∠BED = 90°

m∠5 = _____

$\overset{\frown}{AB}$ = _____ $\overline{AC}$ is a diameter.

$\overset{\frown}{BDA}$ = _____

15. m ∠7 = m ∠8 = 70°

m ∠9 = _____

$\overset{\frown}{CD}$ = _____

$\overline{AC}$ and $\overline{BD}$ are diameters.

Name _____   Date _____

Arcs and Angles

Fill in the blanks.

16. The measure of a minor arc _____ the measure of the central angle that intercepts it.

17. A complete rotation has a measure of _____ degrees.

18. A _____ measures 180°.

19. The measure of a major arc equals 360° minus the measure of the _____ angle that intercepts it.

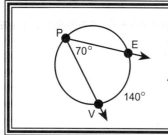

An **inscribed** angle has its vertex on the circle and its sides form chords of the circle. Inscribed ∠VPE intercepts $\overset{\frown}{VE}$.

$$m \angle VPE = \tfrac{1}{2} m \overset{\frown}{VE}$$

Name the arc intercepted by the given angle.

20. ∠LMB   22. ∠LBV   24. ∠MLB   26. ∠BLV

21. ∠MBV   23. ∠BVL   25. ∠MBL   27. ∠MLV

Find the measures of the indicated arcs and angles.

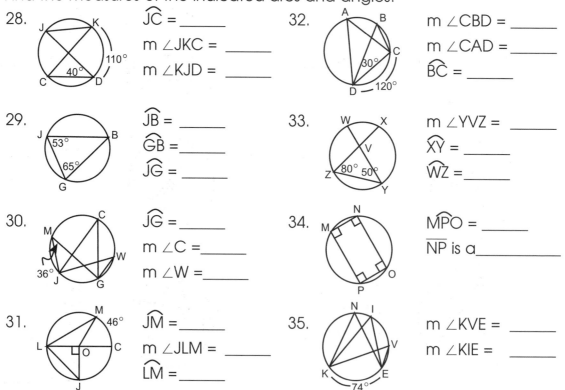

28. $\overset{\frown}{JC}$ = _____
   m ∠JKC = _____
   m ∠KJD = _____

32. m ∠CBD = _____
   m ∠CAD = _____
   $\overset{\frown}{BC}$ = _____

29. $\overset{\frown}{JB}$ = _____
   $\overset{\frown}{GB}$ = _____
   $\overset{\frown}{JG}$ = _____

33. m ∠YVZ = _____
   $\overset{\frown}{XY}$ = _____
   $\overset{\frown}{WZ}$ = _____

30. $\overset{\frown}{JG}$ = _____
   m ∠C = _____
   m ∠W = _____

34. $\overset{\frown}{MPO}$ = _____
   $\overline{NP}$ is a _____

31. $\overset{\frown}{JM}$ = _____
   m ∠JLM = _____
   $\overset{\frown}{LM}$ = _____

35. m ∠KVE = _____
   m ∠KIE = _____

Arcs and Chords

Two chords of a circle are congruent if they intercept congruent arcs.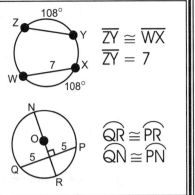

$\overline{ZY} \cong \overline{WX}$
$\overline{ZY} = 7$

Two arcs of a circle are congruent if their chords are congruent.

$\overset{\frown}{QR} \cong \overset{\frown}{PR}$
$\overset{\frown}{QN} \cong \overset{\frown}{PN}$

The perpendicular bisector of a chord of a circle contains the center of the circle and bisects the arcs of chord.

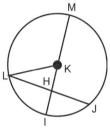

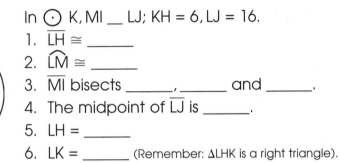

In $\odot$ K, MI __ LJ; KH = 6, LJ = 16.

1. $\overline{LH} \cong$ _____

2. $\overset{\frown}{LM} \cong$ _____

3. $\overline{MI}$ bisects _____, _____ and _____.

4. The midpoint of $\overline{LJ}$ is _____.

5. LH = _____

6. LK = _____ (Remember: $\triangle LHK$ is a right triangle).

Find the arc measures and segment lengths indicated.

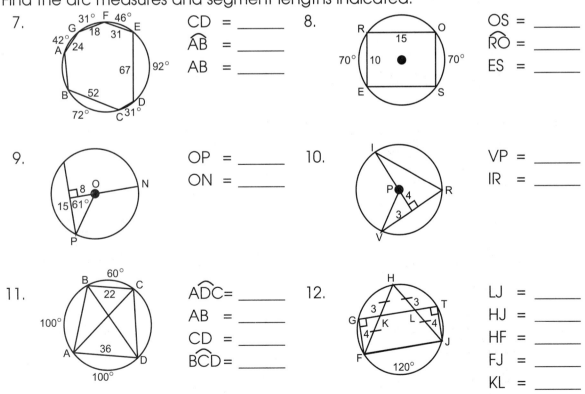

7. CD = _____
    $\overset{\frown}{AB}$ = _____
    AB = _____

8. OS = _____
    $\overset{\frown}{RO}$ = _____
    ES = _____

9. OP = _____
    ON = _____

10. VP = _____
    IR = _____

11. $\overset{\frown}{ADC}$ = _____
    AB = _____
    CD = _____
    $\overset{\frown}{BCD}$ = _____

12. LJ = _____
    HJ = _____
    HF = _____
    FJ = _____
    KL = _____

Lengths of Segments in a Circle

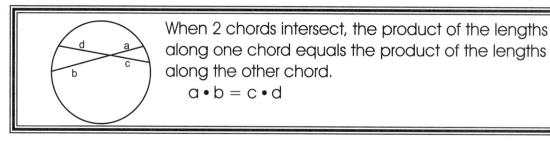

When 2 chords intersect, the product of the lengths along one chord equals the product of the lengths along the other chord.

$$a \cdot b = c \cdot d$$

Find the indicated lengths.

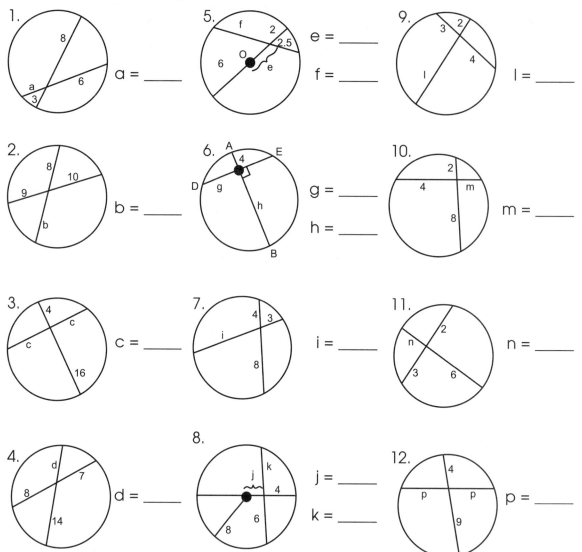

1. $a =$ _____

5. $e =$ _____

     $f =$ _____

9. $l =$ _____

2. $b =$ _____

6. $g =$ _____

     $h =$ _____

10. $m =$ _____

3. $c =$ _____

7. $i =$ _____

11. $n =$ _____

4. $d =$ _____

8. $j =$ _____

     $k =$ _____

12. $p =$ _____

The Earth's equator is a great circle. The diameter of the Earth at the equator is approximately 7926 miles. Substitute the values of the letters into the following to check your work.

$$(A \times B \times C) \times ((D \times E) + F) - (G \times H \times I) - ((J + K) \times (L + M + N)) - P = 7926$$

$$(\_\times\_\times\_) \times ((\_\times\_) +\_) - (\_\times\_\times\_) - ((\_+\_) \times (\_+\_+\_)) -\_ = 7926$$

Mixed Practice with Circles

Find the indicated parts.

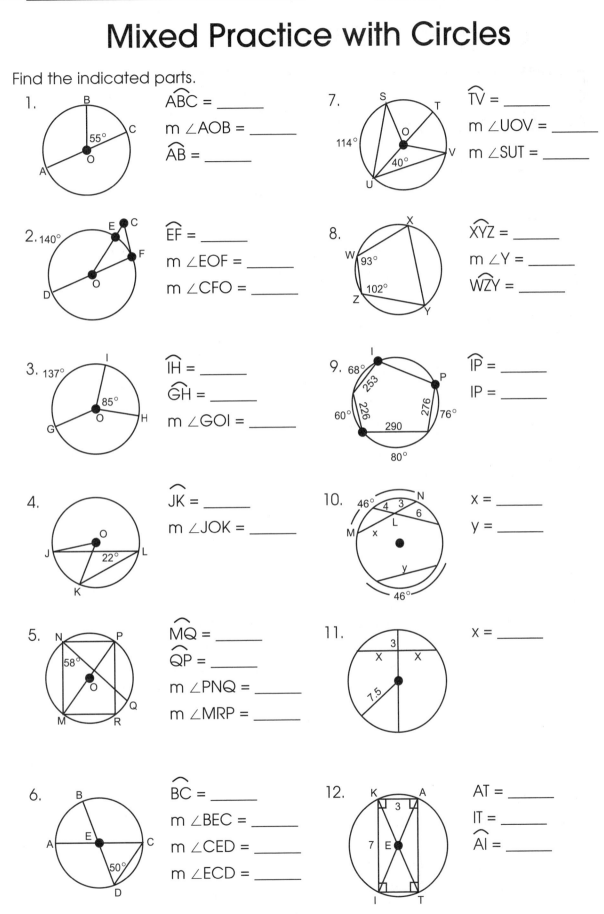

1.
$\overset{\frown}{ABC}$ = _____
m ∠AOB = _____
$\overset{\frown}{AB}$ = _____

7.
$\overset{\frown}{TV}$ = _____
m ∠UOV = _____
m ∠SUT = _____

2.
$\overset{\frown}{EF}$ = _____
m ∠EOF = _____
m ∠CFO = _____

8.
$\overset{\frown}{XYZ}$ = _____
m ∠Y = _____
$\overset{\frown}{WZY}$ = _____

3.
$\overset{\frown}{IH}$ = _____
$\overset{\frown}{GH}$ = _____
m ∠GOI = _____

9.
$\overset{\frown}{IP}$ = _____
IP = _____

4.
$\overset{\frown}{JK}$ = _____
m ∠JOK = _____

10.
x = _____
y = _____

5.
$\overset{\frown}{MQ}$ = _____
$\overset{\frown}{QP}$ = _____
m ∠PNQ = _____
m ∠MRP = _____

11.
x = _____

6.
$\overset{\frown}{BC}$ = _____
m ∠BEC = _____
m ∠CED = _____
m ∠ECD = _____

12.
AT = _____
IT = _____
$\overset{\frown}{AI}$ = _____

Fun Quiz

1. What do you call a man who spent all summer at the beach?

2. What do you say when you see an empty parrot cage?

3. What do you call a crushed angle?

4. What did the Italian say when the witch doctor removed the curse?

5. What did the little acorn say when he grew up?

6. The paper boy delivered papers in a path as follows:
   2 blocks north, 2 blocks east, 2 blocks south and 2 blocks west.
   What did he call his area?

7. What do you call an angle which is adorable?

8. What do you use to tie up a package?

9. What do you call a fierce beast?

10. What do you call more than one L ?

11. What do you call an angle that is never wrong?

12. What do you call people who are in favor of tractors?

13. What do you call a sharp weapon?

14. What do you call the person in charge?

15. What should you do when it rains?

Perimeter

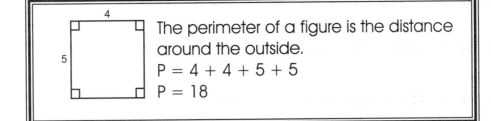

The perimeter of a figure is the distance around the outside.
P = 4 + 4 + 5 + 5
P = 18

Find the perimeter.

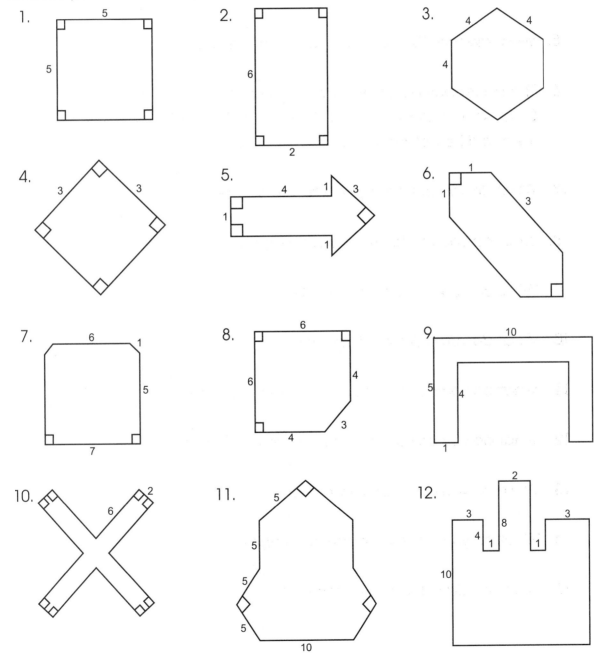

Perimeters and Ratios

In similar figures, the ratio of the perimeter is equal to the ratio of any pair of sides.

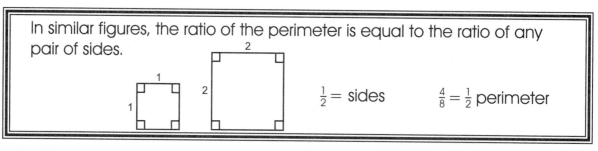

$\frac{1}{2} =$ sides $\frac{4}{8} = \frac{1}{2}$ perimeter

Find the missing perimeter, ratio or labeled side. (All figures are similar.)

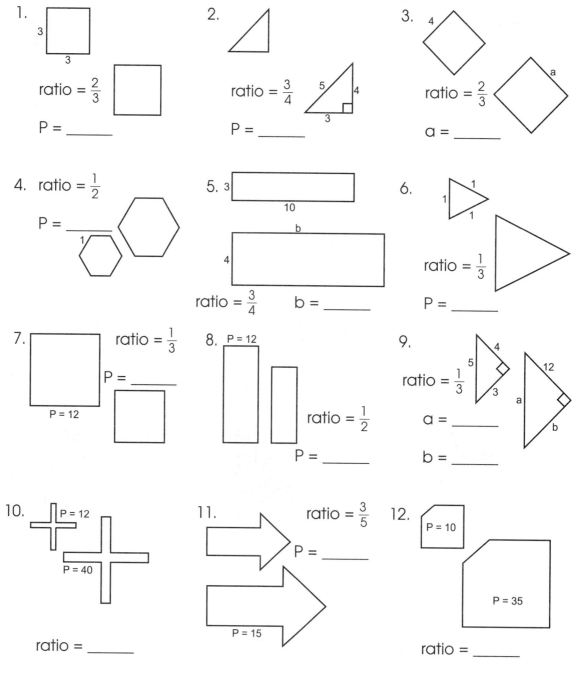

1.   ratio $= \frac{2}{3}$

P = _____

2.   ratio $= \frac{3}{4}$

P = _____

3.   ratio $= \frac{2}{3}$

a = _____

4.   ratio $= \frac{1}{2}$

P = _____

5.   ratio $= \frac{3}{4}$ b = _____

6.   ratio $= \frac{1}{3}$

P = _____

7.   ratio $= \frac{1}{3}$

P = _____

8.   ratio $= \frac{1}{2}$

P = _____

9.   ratio $= \frac{1}{3}$

a = _____

b = _____

10.   ratio = _____

11.   ratio $= \frac{3}{5}$

P = _____

12.   ratio = _____

Area – By Any Other Name

Let each ■ represent 1 square unit. Find the area of each letter, then calculate the area of your name.

1. 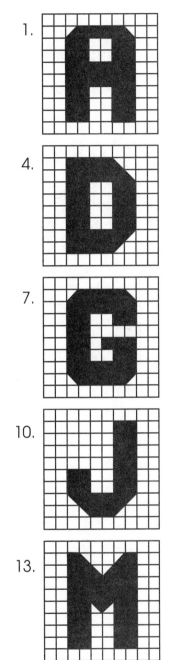 2. 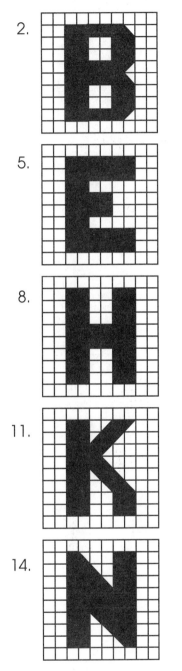 3.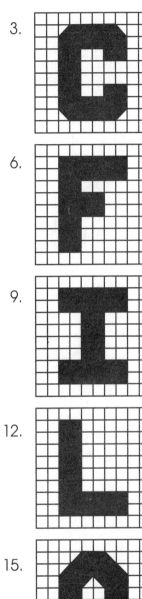

4. 5. 6.

7. 8. 9.

10. 11. 12.

13. 14. 15.

Area – By Any Other Name

Let each ■ represent 1 square unit. Find the area of each letter, then calculate the area of your name.

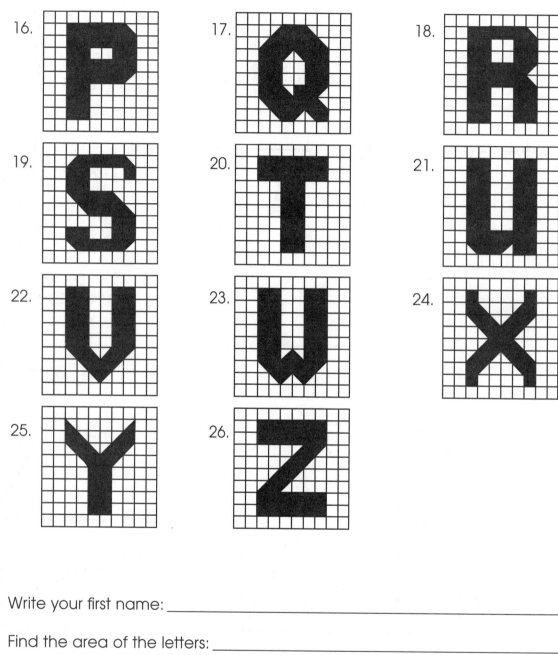

Write your first name: _____

Find the area of the letters: _____

Write your last name: _____

Find the area of the letters: _____

Name _____   Date _____

Square Units

> Area is measured in square units.
>
> 8 units²
>
> 8 units²

Find the area of the figures shown.

Rectangles and Squares

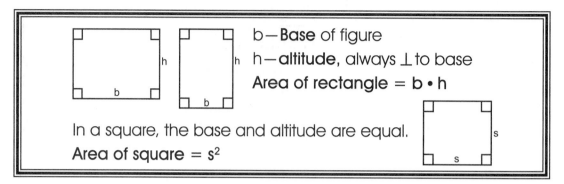

b—**Base** of figure

h—**altitude**, always ⊥ to base

Area of rectangle = b • h

In a square, the base and altitude are equal.

Area of square = s²

Find the area of each square or rectangle.

1. 6 cm 12 cm

3. 2.7 in. 1.3 in.

5. 1.1 ft. 1.1 ft.

2. 9 cm 9 cm

4. 4½ cm 8½ cm

6. 1 cm 25 cm

Find the the total area of each figure: 1) Divide each figure into rectangles; 2) Find the area of each rectangle; 3) Add the areas.

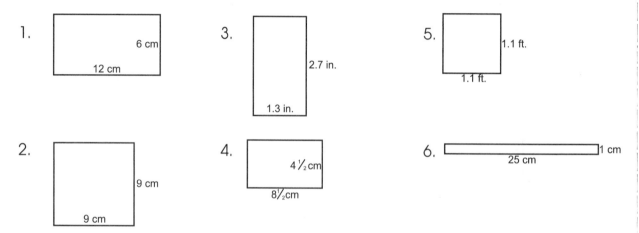

7. 2 4 6 9 5 8

8. 3 9 9 9 3 3

9. 18 4 7 20 6 2 17

Find the area of the shaded region.

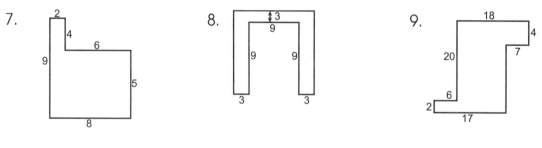

10. 5 2 6 11

11. 4 5 3 5

12. 6 1 5 10 14 5 1 6 8

Area: Parallelograms and Triangles

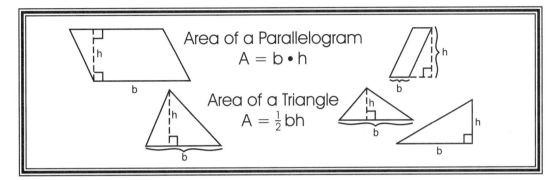

Area of a Parallelogram
$$A = b \cdot h$$

Area of a Triangle
$$A = \tfrac{1}{2}bh$$

Find the area of each parallelogram or triangle.

1.
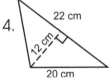

5.
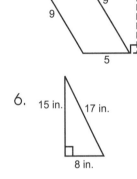

9.
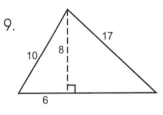

2.
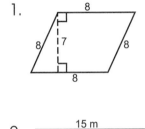

6.
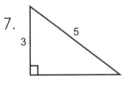

10.
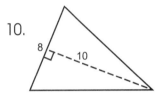

3.
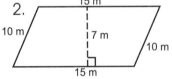

7.
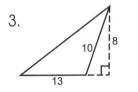

11.
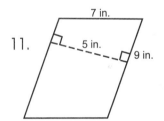

4.
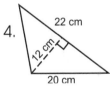

8.
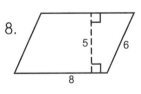

12.
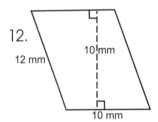

Find the area of the shaded region.

13.
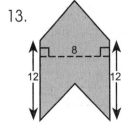

14.
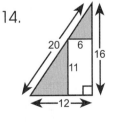

15.
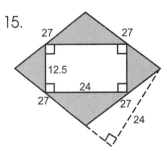

Name _____ Date _____

Area: Trapezoids

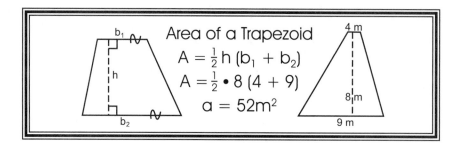

Area of a Trapezoid
$$A = \tfrac{1}{2} h (b_1 + b_2)$$
$$A = \tfrac{1}{2} \cdot 8 (4 + 9)$$
$$a = 52m^2$$

Find the area of each trapezoid.

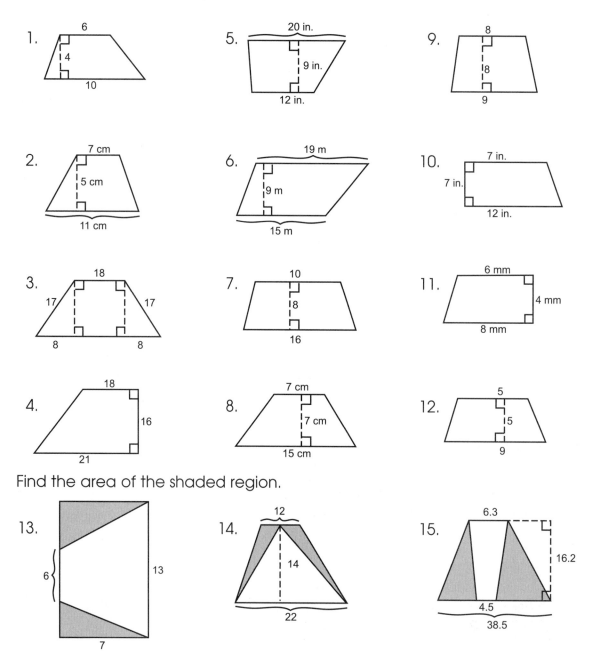

1. 6 / 4 / 10

2. 7 cm / 5 cm / 11 cm

3. 18 / 17 / 17 / 8 / 8

4. 18 / 16 / 21

5. 20 in. / 9 in. / 12 in.

6. 19 m / 9 m / 15 m

7. 10 / 8 / 16

8. 7 cm / 7 cm / 15 cm

9. 8 / 8 / 9

10. 7 in. / 7 in. / 12 in.

11. 6 mm / 4 mm / 8 mm

12. 5 / 5 / 9

Find the area of the shaded region.

13. 6 / 13 / 7

14. 12 / 14 / 22

15. 6.3 / 16.2 / 4.5 / 38.5

Name _____   Date _____

Circumference of a Circle

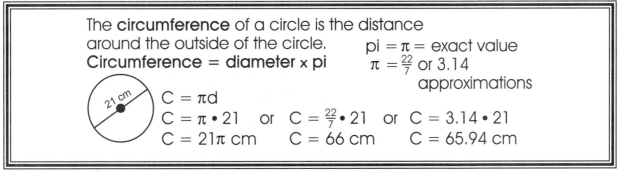

The **circumference** of a circle is the distance
around the outside of the circle.   pi = π = exact value
Circumference = diameter x pi $\pi = \frac{22}{7}$ or 3.14
                                                          approximations

$C = \pi d$
$C = \pi \cdot 21$ or $C = \frac{22}{7} \cdot 21$ or $C = 3.14 \cdot 21$
$C = 21\pi$ cm $C = 66$ cm $C = 65.94$ cm

Find the circumference using the indicated value for pi.

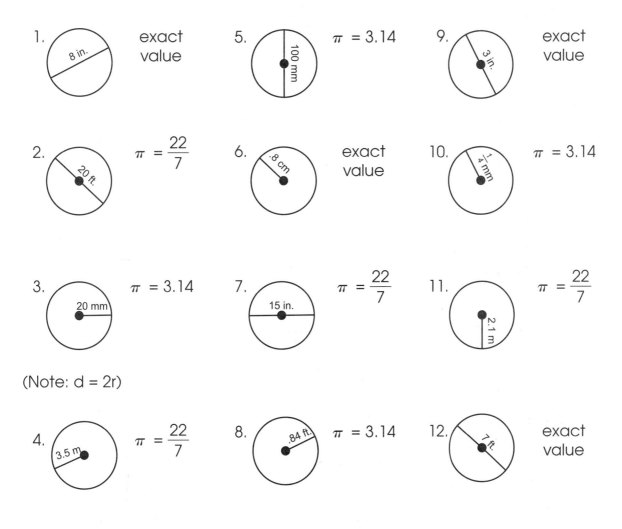

1. 8 in.   exact value

2. 20 ft. $\pi = \frac{22}{7}$

3. 20 mm $\pi = 3.14$

(Note: d = 2r)

4. 3.5 m $\pi = \frac{22}{7}$

5. 100 mm $\pi = 3.14$

6. .8 cm   exact value

7. 15 in. $\pi = \frac{22}{7}$

8. .84 ft. $\pi = 3.14$

9. 3 in.   exact value

10. $\frac{1}{4}$ mm $\pi = 3.14$

11. 2.1 m $\pi = \frac{22}{7}$

12. 7 ft.   exact value

13. The wheel of a wagon has a radius of 4.9 inches. How far does the wagon
     travel in one turn of he wheel? ($\pi = \frac{22}{7}$)

Name _____   Date _____

Area of a Circle

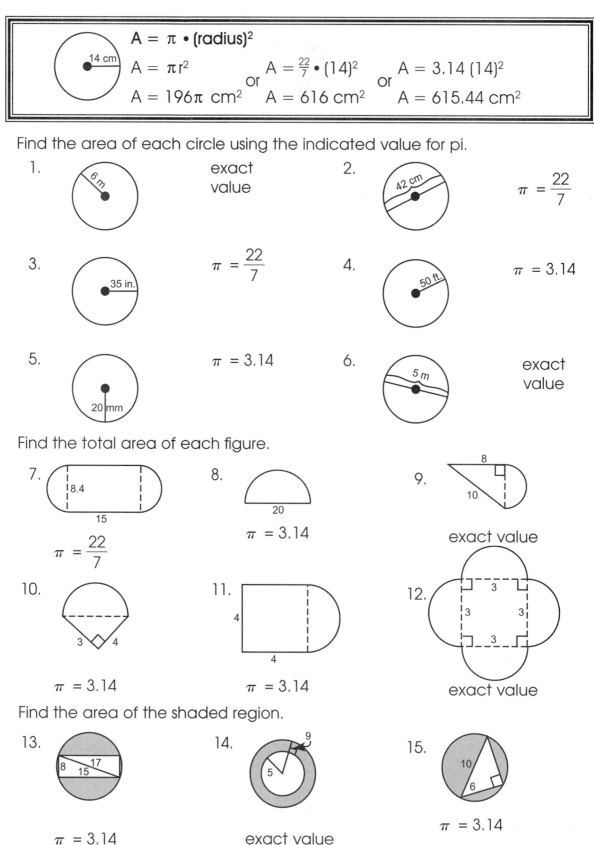

$A = \pi \cdot (radius)^2$

$A = \pi r^2$ or $A = \frac{22}{7} \cdot (14)^2$ or $A = 3.14\,(14)^2$

$A = 196\pi$ cm² $A = 616$ cm² $A = 615.44$ cm²

(14 cm)

Find the area of each circle using the indicated value for pi.

1. 6 m   exact value

2. 42 cm $\pi = \frac{22}{7}$

3. 35 in. $\pi = \frac{22}{7}$

4. 50 ft. $\pi = 3.14$

5. 20 mm $\pi = 3.14$

6. 5 m   exact value

Find the total area of each figure.

7. 8.4   15 $\pi = \frac{22}{7}$

8. 20 $\pi = 3.14$

9. 8   10   exact value

10. 3   4 $\pi = 3.14$

11. 4   4 $\pi = 3.14$

12. 3   3   3   3   exact value

exact value

Find the area of the shaded region.

13. 8   17   15 $\pi = 3.14$

14. 9   5   exact value

15. 10   6 $\pi = 3.14$

Name _____   Date _____

Tracing Fun

Draw each figure without lifting your pencil from the paper and without tracing any line more than once. Start at the dot.

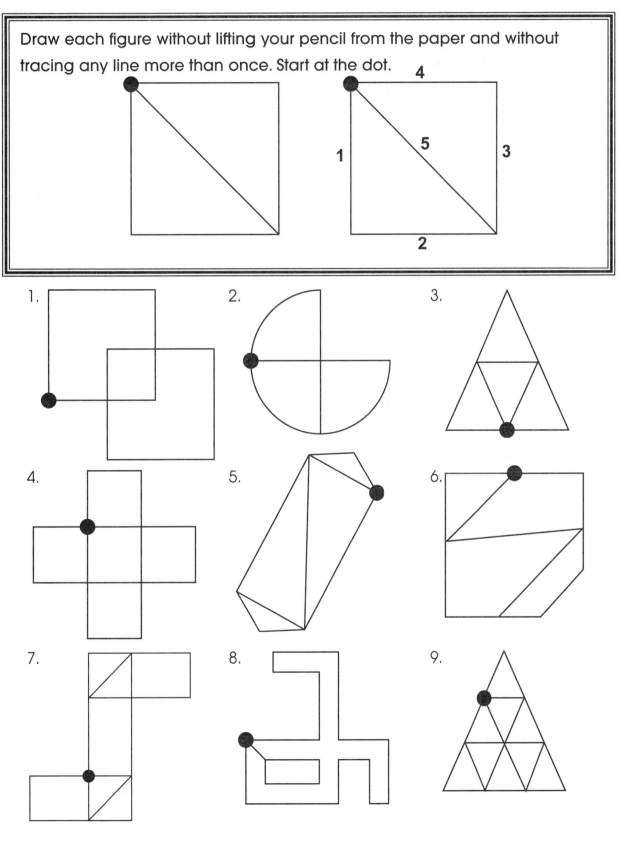

1.

2.

3.

4.

5.

6.

7.

8.

9.

Name _____   Date _____

Network News

Network terms:
Network – graphical system of points called vertices
Edges – segments connecting the vertices
Degree of a vertex – number of edges that meet at the vertex
Traceable network – can start at a vertex and travel to all other vertices
along each edge exactly once.

For each network, state the number of vertices (V) and the number of
edges (E).

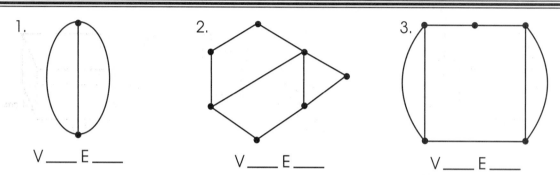

1. V ___ E ___

2. V ___ E ___

3. V ___ E ___

To trace a network, you must be able to "enter" and "leave" each vertex – an
even degree – except perhaps the starting and ending vertices. Therefore, a
network is traceable if it has no more than two vertices of odd degree.

Next to each vertex write the degree. If the network is traceable, list the order
of the vertices for a possible trace.

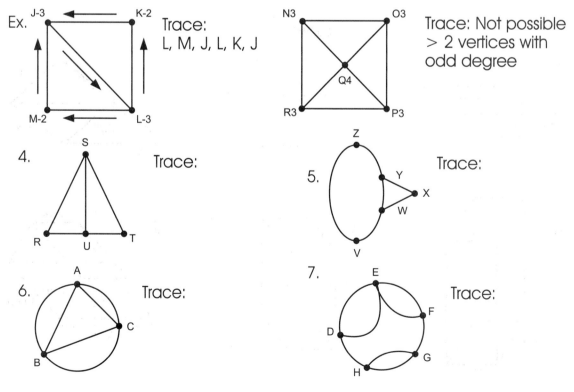

Ex.   Trace:
      L, M, J, L, K, J

Trace: Not possible
> 2 vertices with
odd degree

4. Trace:

5. Trace:

6. Trace:

7. Trace:

Surface Area of Rectangular Prisms

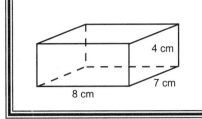

There are 6 rectangular sides or faces.
Opposite sides are parallel and congruent.
Surface area—Find the area of each
face and add.
SA = 8•4+7•4+8•4+7•4+8•7+8•7 = 232 cm²

Find the surface area of each prism.

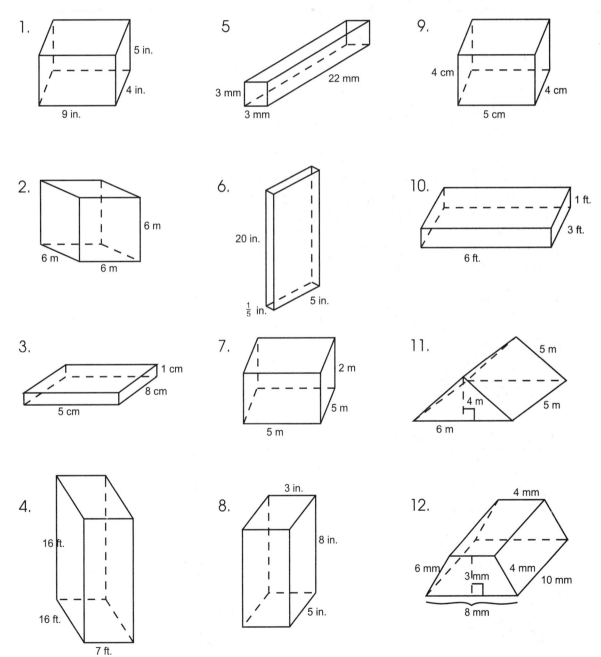

1.
5 in.
4 in.
9 in.

5
22 mm
3 mm
3 mm

9.
4 cm
4 cm
5 cm

2.
6 m
6 m
6 m

6.
20 in.
$\frac{1}{5}$ in.
5 in.

10.
1 ft.
3 ft.
6 ft.

3.
1 cm
8 cm
5 cm

7.
2 m
5 m
5 m

11.
5 m
4 m
5 m
6 m

4.
16 ft.
16 ft.
7 ft.

8.
3 in.
8 in.
5 in.

12.
4 mm
6 mm
3 mm
4 mm
10 mm
8 mm

Volume of Prisms

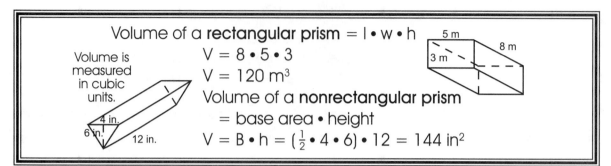

Volume of a **rectangular prism** = l • w • h

V = 8 • 5 • 3

V = 120 m³

Volume is measured in cubic units.

Volume of a **nonrectangular prism**
= base area • height
V = B • h = ($\frac{1}{2}$ • 4 • 6) • 12 = 144 in²

Find the volume of each prism.

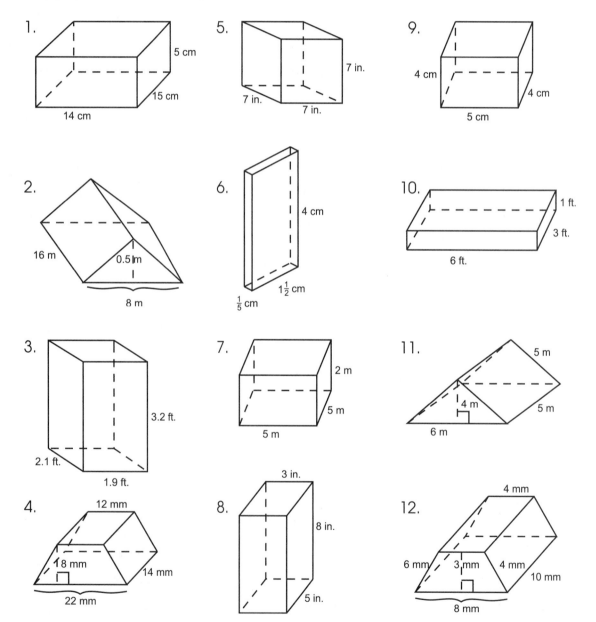

1. 5 cm, 15 cm, 14 cm

2. 16 m, 0.5 m, 8 m

3. 3.2 ft., 2.1 ft., 1.9 ft.

4. 12 mm, 8 mm, 14 mm, 22 mm

5. 7 in., 7 in., 7 in.

6. 4 cm, $1\frac{1}{2}$ cm, $\frac{1}{5}$ cm

7. 2 m, 5 m, 5 m

8. 3 in., 8 in., 5 in.

9. 4 cm, 4 cm, 5 cm

10. 1 ft., 3 ft., 6 ft.

11. 5 m, 4 m, 5 m, 6 m

12. 4 mm, 6 mm, 3 mm, 4 mm, 10 mm, 8 mm

Surface Area of Cylinders

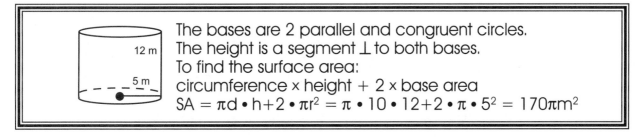

The bases are 2 parallel and congruent circles.
The height is a segment ⊥ to both bases.
To find the surface area:
circumference × height + 2 × base area
$SA = \pi d \cdot h + 2 \cdot \pi r^2 = \pi \cdot 10 \cdot 12 + 2 \cdot \pi \cdot 5^2 = 170\pi m^2$

Find the surface area of each cylinder using the indicated value for pi.

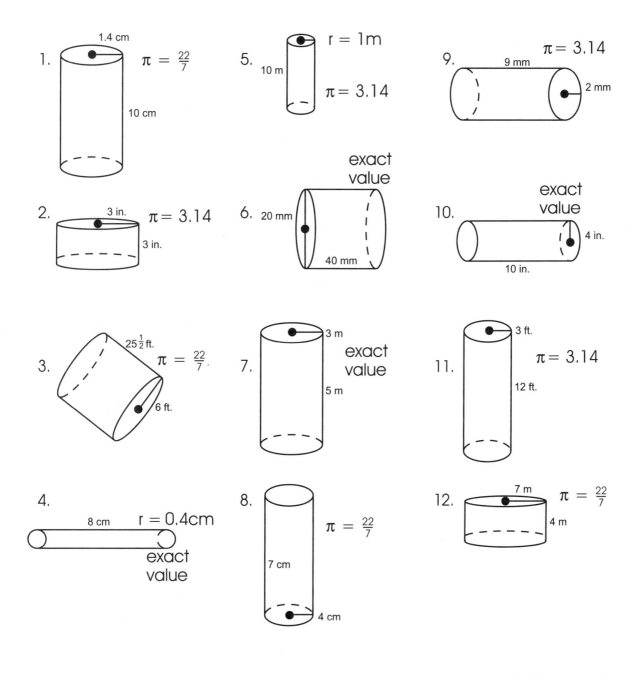

1. 1.4 cm $\pi = \frac{22}{7}$ 10 cm

2. 3 in. $\pi = 3.14$ 3 in.

3. $25\frac{1}{2}$ ft. $\pi = \frac{22}{7}$ 6 ft.

4. 8 cm r = 0.4cm exact value

5. r = 1m 10 m $\pi = 3.14$

6. 20 mm 40 mm exact value

7. 3 m 5 m exact value

8. 7 cm 4 cm $\pi = \frac{22}{7}$

9. $\pi = 3.14$ 9 mm 2 mm

10. exact value 10 in. 4 in.

11. 3 ft. 12 ft. $\pi = 3.14$

12. 7 m 4 m $\pi = \frac{22}{7}$

Volume of Cylinders

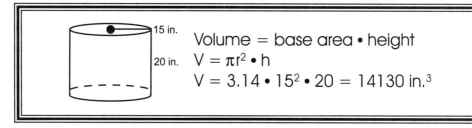

Volume = base area • height
$V = \pi r^2 \cdot h$
$V = 3.14 \cdot 15^2 \cdot 20 = 14130 \text{ in.}^3$

Find the volume using the indicated value for pi.

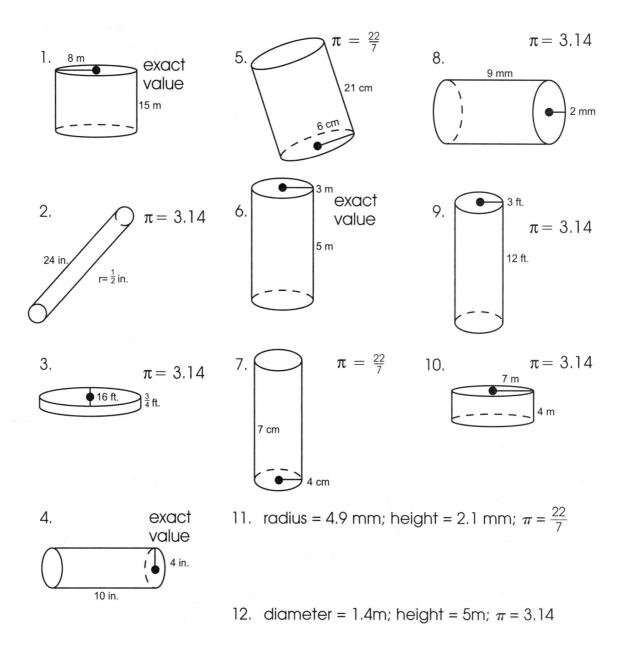

1. 8 m   exact value   15 m

2. $\pi = 3.14$ 24 in. $r = \frac{1}{2}$ in.

3. $\pi = 3.14$ 16 ft. $\frac{3}{4}$ ft.

4. exact value   4 in.   10 in.

5. $\pi = \frac{22}{7}$ 21 cm   6 cm

6. 3 m   exact value   5 m

7. $\pi = \frac{22}{7}$ 7 cm   4 cm

8. $\pi = 3.14$ 9 mm   2 mm

9. 3 ft. $\pi = 3.14$ 12 ft.

10. $\pi = 3.14$ 7 m   4 m

11. radius = 4.9 mm; height = 2.1 mm; $\pi = \frac{22}{7}$

12. diameter = 1.4m; height = 5m; $\pi = 3.14$

Mixed Practice with Area and Volume

Find the area of the shaded region.

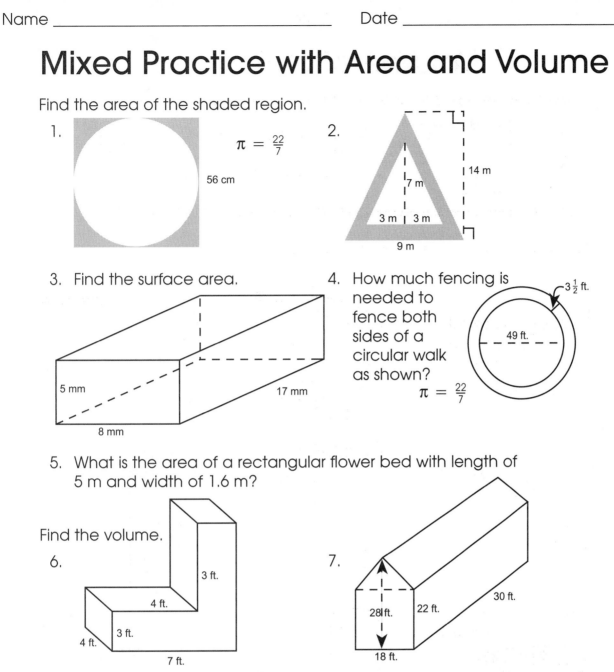

1.

56 cm

$\pi = \frac{22}{7}$

2.

14 m

7 m

3 m | 3 m

9 m

3. Find the surface area.

5 mm

17 mm

8 mm

4. How much fencing is needed to fence both sides of a circular walk as shown?

$\pi = \frac{22}{7}$

$3\frac{1}{2}$ ft.

49 ft.

5. What is the area of a rectangular flower bed with length of 5 m and width of 1.6 m?

Find the volume.

6.

3 ft.

4 ft.

3 ft.

4 ft.

7 ft.

7.

28 ft.

22 ft.

30 ft.

18 ft.

8. A dress pattern requires a triangular-shaped piece with a 10 in. base and an 18 in. height. Find the area of the piece.

9. A water trough is half of a circular cylinder with a 6 ft. radius and a 3 ft. height. Find the volume. $\pi = 3.14$.

10. A doghouse is a cube with sides of length 5 feet. How much wood is needed if it does not have a floor? What is the volume?

11. A nightstand has a base $1\frac{1}{2}$ ft. by 2 ft. and a height of 3 ft. How much space does it need on the floor? What is the volume?

STATEly Areas

Calculate the area of each state.
Measures are approximate.

Wyoming:

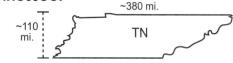

1. Wyoming resembles a

   _____

2. The area formula is A =

   _____

3. The area of Wyoming =

   _____

Tennessee:

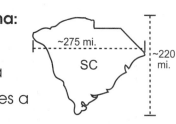

4. Tennessee resembles a

   _____

5. The area formula is A =

   _____

6. The area of Tennessee =

   _____

South Carolina:

7. South Carolina resembles a

   _____

8. The area formula is A =

   _____

9. The area of South Carolina =

   _____

Missouri:

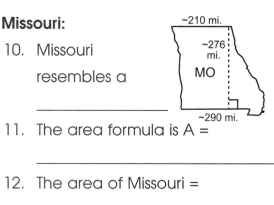

10. Missouri resembles a

    _____

11. The area formula is A =

    _____

12. The area of Missouri =

    _____

Subdivide the states into 2 geometric shapes to help calculate the total area.

Utah:

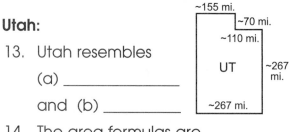

13. Utah resembles

    (a) _____

    and (b) _____

14. The area formulas are

    (a) A = _____ and (b) A = _____

15. The area of Utah =

    _____ + _____ = _____

Nevada:

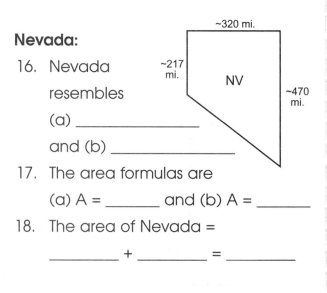

16. Nevada resembles

    (a) _____

    and (b) _____

17. The area formulas are

    (a) A = _____ and (b) A = _____

18. The area of Nevada =

    _____ + _____ = _____

Surface Area of Pyramids

There are 4 triangular faces and a rectangular base.

Surface area—Find the area of each face and add.

$$SA = 6 \cdot 6 + 4 \left(\tfrac{1}{2}\right) (6) (5) = 96 \text{ cm}^2$$

Surface area is measured in square units.

Find the surface area of each pyramid.

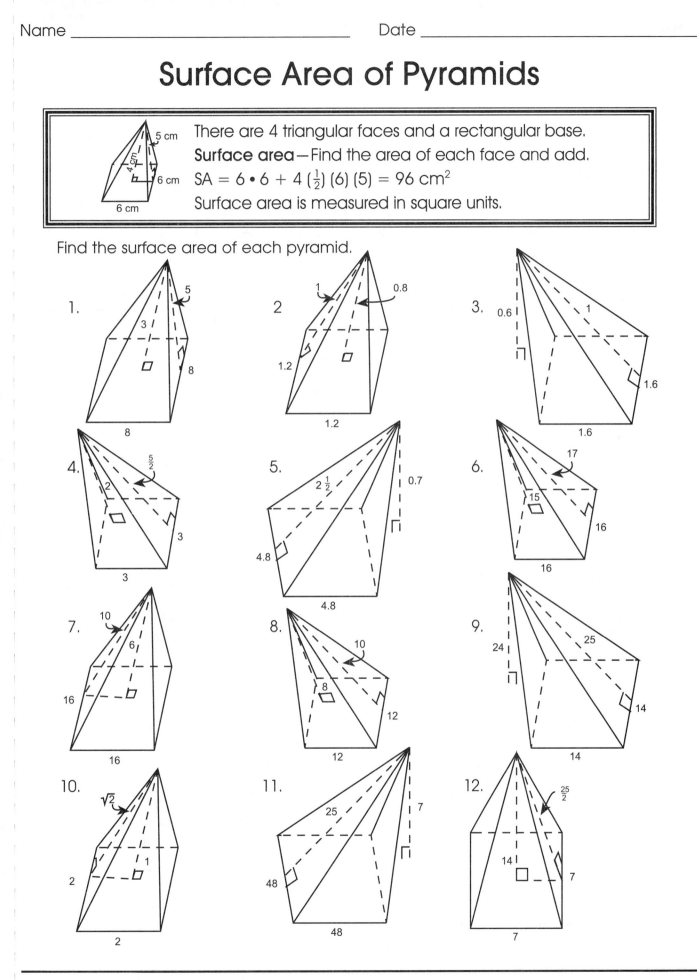

1. 5, 3, 8, 8

2. 1, 0.8, 1.2, 1.2

3. 0.6, 1, 1.6, 1.6

4. $\frac{5}{2}$, 2, 3, 3

5. $2\frac{1}{2}$, 0.7, 4.8, 4.8

6. 17, 15, 16, 16

7. 10, 6, 16, 16

8. 10, 8, 12, 12

9. 24, 25, 14, 14

10. $\sqrt{2}$, 1, 2, 2

11. 25, 7, 48, 48

12. $\frac{25}{2}$, 14, 7, 7

Volume of Pyramids

Volume of a pyramid = $\frac{1}{3}$ • (area of base) • (height)

$V = \frac{1}{3} • (6 • 6) • (4)$

$V = 48$ cm^2

Volume is measured in cubic units.

Find the volume of each pyramid.

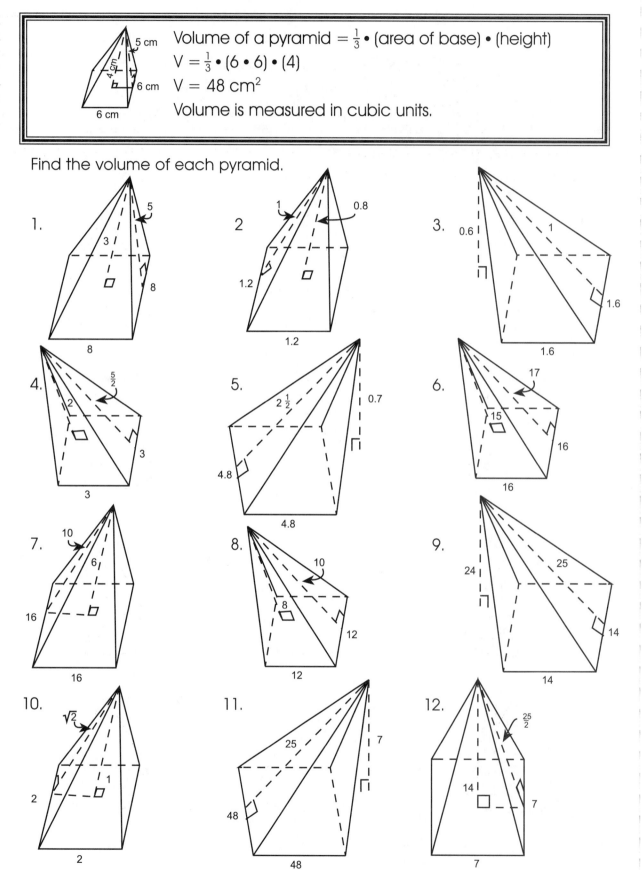

Surface Area of Right Circular Cones

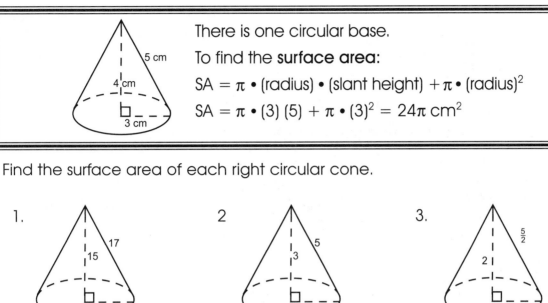

There is one circular base.

To find the **surface area**:

SA = π • (radius) • (slant height) + π • (radius)²

SA = π • (3) (5) + π • (3)² = 24π cm²

Find the surface area of each right circular cone.

1.

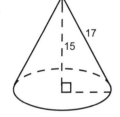

17
15

2

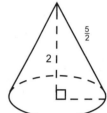

5
3

3.

$\frac{5}{2}$
2

4.

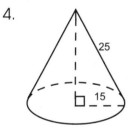

25
15

5.

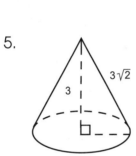

$3\sqrt{2}$
3

6.

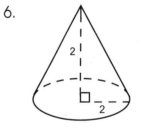

2
2

7.

10
6

8.

2
1

9.

7
5

10.

7
3

11.

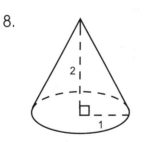

25
7

12.

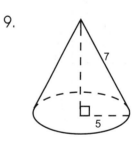

12
9

About the Authors

Mary Lee Vivian has helped many secondary students master a variety of mathematical skills during her many years of teaching in the Parkway School District in St. Louis, Missouri. She holds a bachelor of arts degree in mathematics from Central Methodist College and a master's degree from the University of Missouri – St. Louis.

Tammy Bohn-Voepel is currently working on a master of science and a doctor of philosophy in mathematics degree at the University of Missouri. She holds a bachelor of science and a bachelor of arts degree in mathematics and a master of arts in education, each from Northeast Missouri State University.,

Margaret Thomas is currently a mathematics and science consultant for a major publisher. Her professional experience includes teaching mathematics grades seven through college in Ohio, California, Oklahoma, and Tennessee. For ten years, she served as the Mathematics-Science Coordinator K-12 for Putnam City Schools in Oklahoma City. Margaret is an active member of many professional organizations including NCTM. She currently lives in Indianapolis, Indiana.

Answer Key

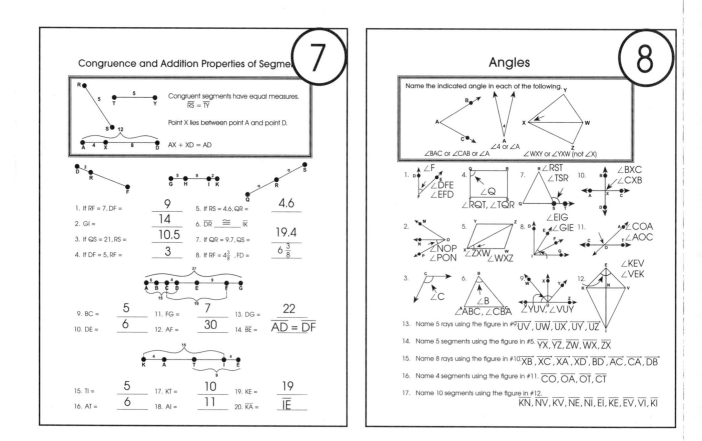

Answer Key

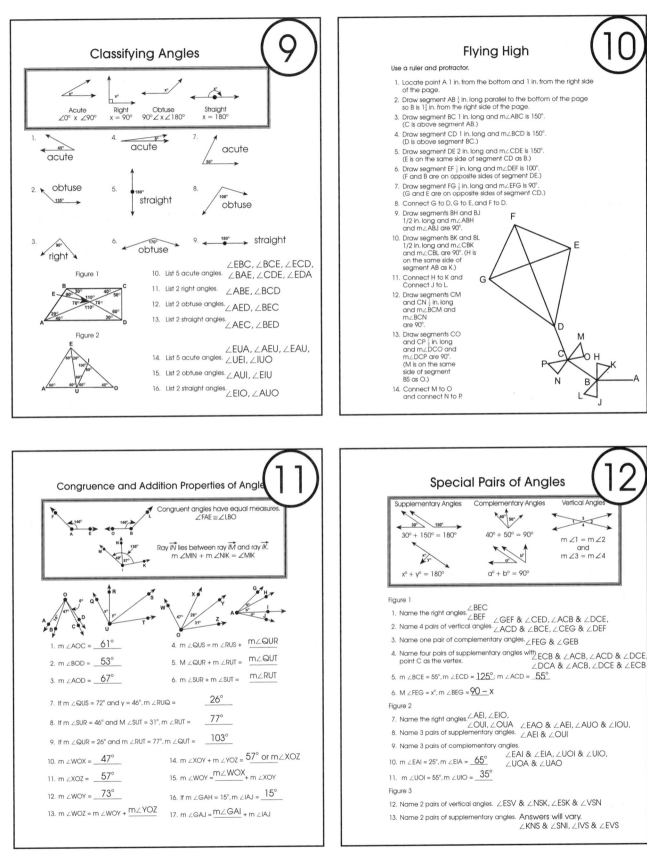

Classifying Angles ⑨

Acute ∠0° x ∠90° **Right** x = 90° **Obtuse** 90°∠ x ∠180° **Straight** x = 180°

1. 45° acute
2. 135° obtuse
3. 90° right
4. acute
5. 180° straight
6. 170° obtuse
7. 50° acute
8. 108° obtuse
9. 180° straight

Figure 1

10. List 5 acute angles. ∠EBC, ∠BCE, ∠ECD, ∠BAE, ∠CDE, ∠EDA
11. List 2 right angles. ∠ABE, ∠BCD
12. List 2 obtuse angles. ∠AED, ∠BEC
13. List 2 straight angles. ∠AEC, ∠BED

Figure 2

14. List 5 acute angles. ∠EUA, ∠AEU, ∠EAU, ∠UEI, ∠IUO
15. List 2 obtuse angles. ∠AUI, ∠EIU
16. List 2 straight angles. ∠EIO, ∠AUO

Flying High ⑩

Use a ruler and protractor.

1. Locate point A 1 in. from the bottom and 1 in. from the right side of the page.
2. Draw segment AB ¾ in. long parallel to the bottom of the page so B is 1¾ in. from the right side of the page.
3. Draw segment BC 1 in. long and m∠ABC is 150°. (C is above segment AB.)
4. Draw segment CD 1 in. long and m∠BCD is 150°. (D is above segment BC.)
5. Draw segment DE 2 in. long and m∠CDE is 150°. (E is on the same side of segment CD as B.)
6. Draw segment EF ½ in. long and m∠DEF is 100°. (F and B are on opposite sides of segment DE.)
7. Draw segment FG ½ in. long and m∠EFG is 90°. (G and E are on opposite sides of segment CD.)
8. Connect G to D, G to E, and F to D.
9. Draw segments BH and BJ 1/2 in. long and m∠ABH and m∠ABJ are 90°.
10. Draw segments BK and BL 1/2 in. long and m∠CBK and m∠CBL are 90°. (H is on the same side of segment AB as K.)
11. Connect H to K and Connect J to L.
12. Draw segments CM and CN ½ in. long and m∠BCM and m∠BCN are 90°.
13. Draw segments CO and CP ½ in. long and m∠DCO and m∠DCP are 90°. (M is on the same side of segment BS as O.)
14. Connect M to O and connect N to P.

Congruence and Addition Properties of Angles ⑪

Congruent angles have equal measures. ∠FAE ≅ ∠LBO

Ray IN lies between ray IM and ray IK. m ∠MIN + m ∠NIK = ∠MIK

1. m ∠AOC = __61°__
2. m ∠BOD = __53°__
3. m ∠AOD = __67°__
4. m ∠QUS = m ∠RUS + __m∠QUR__
5. M ∠QUR + m ∠RUT = __m∠QUT__
6. m ∠SUR + m ∠SUT = __m∠RUT__
7. If m ∠QUS = 72° and y = 46°, m ∠RUQ = __26°__
8. If m ∠SUR = 46° and M ∠SUT = 31°, m ∠RUT = __77°__
9. If m ∠QUR = 26° and m ∠RUT = 77°, m ∠QUT = __103°__
10. m ∠WOX = __47°__
11. m ∠XOZ = __57°__
12. m ∠WOY = __73°__
13. m ∠WOZ = m ∠WOY + __m∠YOZ__
14. m ∠XOY + m ∠YOZ = __57° or m∠XOZ__
15. m ∠WOY = __m∠WOX__ + m ∠XOY
16. If m ∠GAH = 15°, m ∠IAJ = __15°__
17. m ∠GAJ = __m∠GAI__ + m ∠IAJ

Special Pairs of Angles ⑫

Supplementary Angles 30° 150° 30° + 150° = 180° x° + y° = 180°
Complementary Angles 40° 50° 40° + 50° = 90° a° + b° = 90°
Vertical Angles m ∠1 = m ∠2 and m ∠3 = m ∠4

Figure 1
1. Name the right angles. ∠BEC, ∠BEF
2. Name 4 pairs of vertical angles. ∠GEF & ∠CED, ∠ACB & ∠DCE, ∠ACD & ∠BCE, ∠CEG & ∠DEF
3. Name one pair of complementary angles. ∠FEG & ∠GEB
4. Name four pairs of supplementary angles with point C as the vertex. ∠ECB & ∠ACB, ∠ACD & ∠DCE, ∠DCA & ∠ACB, ∠DCE & ∠ECB
5. m ∠BCE = 55°, m ∠ECD = __125°__; m ∠ACD = __55°__
6. M ∠FEG = x°, m ∠BEG = __90 – x__

Figure 2
7. Name the right angles. ∠AEI, ∠EIO, ∠OUI, ∠OUA
8. Name 3 pairs of supplementary angles. ∠EAO & ∠AEI, ∠AUO & ∠IOU, ∠AEI & ∠OUI
9. Name 3 pairs of complementary angles. ∠EAI & ∠EIA, ∠UOI & ∠UIO, ∠UOA & ∠UAO
10. m ∠EAI = 25°, m ∠EIA = __65°__
11. m ∠UOI = 55°, m ∠UIO = __35°__

Figure 3
12. Name 2 pairs of vertical angles. ∠ESV & ∠NSK, ∠ESK & ∠VSN
13. Name 2 pairs of supplementary angles. Answers will vary. ∠KNS & ∠SNI, ∠IVS & ∠EVS

Answer Key

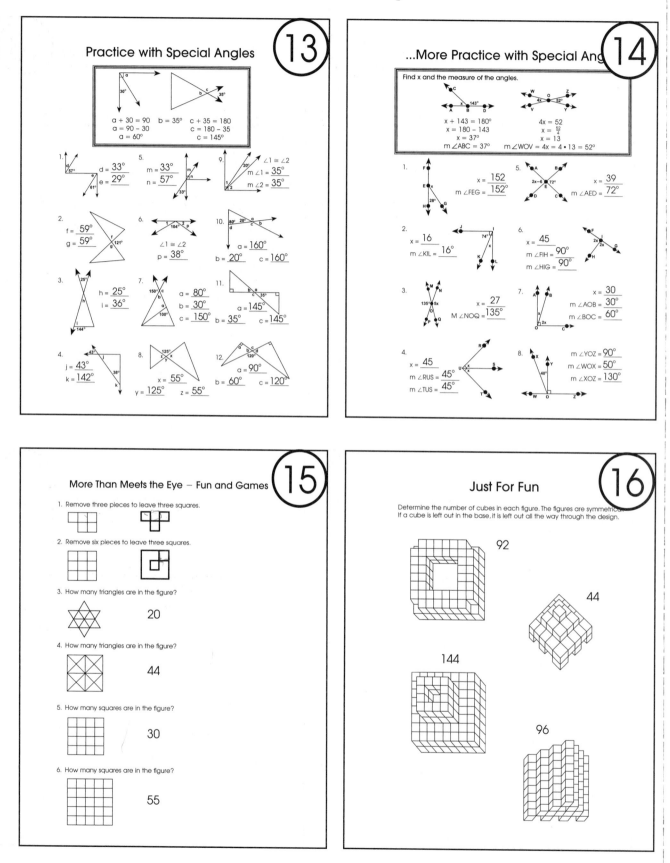

Practice with Special Angles (13)

$$a + 30 = 90 \quad b = 35° \quad c + 35 = 180$$
$$a = 90 - 30 \qquad\qquad c = 180 - 35$$
$$a = 60° \qquad\qquad\qquad c = 145°$$

1. $d = \underline{33°}$
   $e = \underline{29°}$

5. $m = \underline{33°}$
   $n = \underline{57°}$

9. $\angle 1 \cong \angle 2$
   $m \angle 1 = \underline{35°}$
   $m \angle 2 = \underline{35°}$

2. $f = \underline{59°}$
   $g = \underline{59°}$

6. $\angle 1 \cong \angle 2$
   $p = \underline{38°}$

10. $a = \underline{160°}$
    $b = \underline{20°}$ $c = \underline{160°}$

3. $h = \underline{25°}$
   $i = \underline{36°}$

7. $a = \underline{80°}$
   $b = \underline{30°}$
   $c = \underline{150°}$

11. $a = \underline{145°}$
    $b = \underline{35°}$ $c = \underline{145°}$

4. $j = \underline{43°}$
   $k = \underline{142°}$

8. $x = \underline{55°}$
   $y = \underline{125°}$ $z = \underline{55°}$

12. $a = \underline{90°}$
    $b = \underline{60°}$ $c = \underline{120°}$

...More Practice with Special Angles (14)

Find x and the measure of the angles.

$$x + 143 = 180° \qquad 4x = 52$$
$$x = 180 - 143 \qquad x = \tfrac{52}{4}$$
$$x = 37° \qquad\qquad x = 13$$
$$m \angle ABC = 37° \qquad m \angle WOV = 4x = 4 \cdot 13 = 52°$$

1. $x = \underline{152}$
   $m \angle FEG = \underline{152}$

5. $x = \underline{39}$
   $m \angle AED = \underline{72°}$

2. $x = \underline{16}$
   $m \angle KIL = \underline{16°}$

6. $x = \underline{45}$
   $m \angle FIH = \underline{90°}$
   $m \angle HIG = \underline{90°}$

3. $x = \underline{27}$
   $M \angle NOQ = \underline{135°}$

7. $x = \underline{30}$
   $m \angle AOB = \underline{30°}$
   $m \angle BOC = \underline{60°}$

4. $x = \underline{45}$
   $m \angle RUS = \underline{45°}$
   $m \angle TUS = \underline{45°}$

8. $m \angle YOZ = \underline{90°}$
   $m \angle WOX = \underline{50°}$
   $m \angle XOZ = \underline{130°}$

More Than Meets the Eye – Fun and Games (15)

1. Remove three pieces to leave three squares.

2. Remove six pieces to leave three squares.

3. How many triangles are in the figure?   20

4. How many triangles are in the figure?   44

5. How many squares are in the figure?   30

6. How many squares are in the figure?   55

Just For Fun (16)

Determine the number of cubes in each figure. The figures are symmetrical. If a cube is left out in the base, it is left out all the way through the design.

92

44

144

96

Answer Key

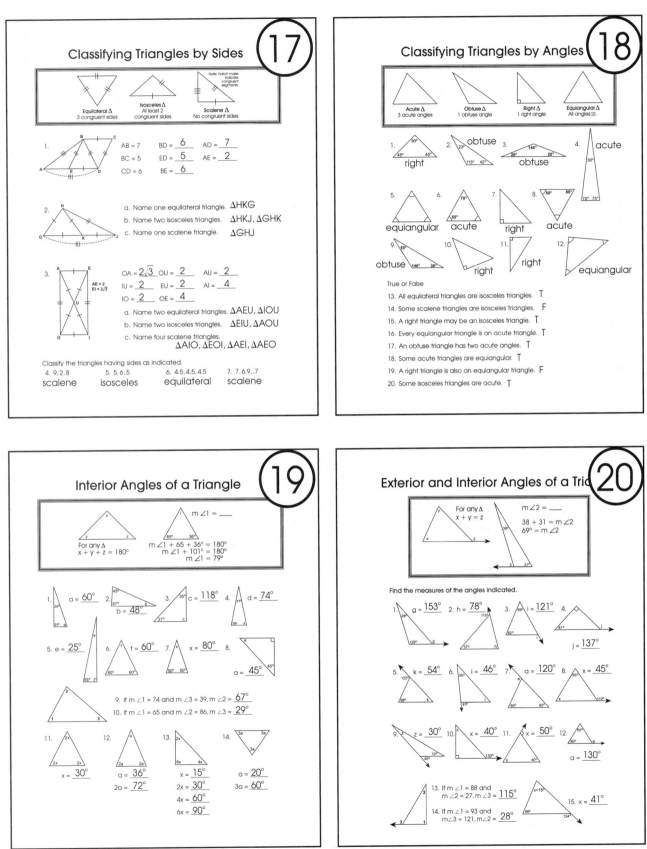

Classifying Triangles by Sides ⑰

Note: hatch marks indicate congruent segments.

Equilateral △ — 3 congruent sides
Isosceles △ — At least 2 congruent sides
Scalene △ — No congruent sides

1. AB = 7   BD = __6__   AD = __7__
    BC = 5   ED = __5__   AE = __2__
    CD = 6   BE = __6__

2. a. Name one equilateral triangle.   △HKG
    b. Name two isosceles triangles.   △HKJ, △GHK
    c. Name one scalene triangle.   △GHJ

3. AE = 2
    EI = 2/3
    OA = $2\sqrt{3}$ OU = __2__   AU = __2__
    IU = __2__   EU = __2__   AI = __4__
    IO = __2__   OE = __4__

    a. Name two equilateral triangles.   △AEU, △IOU
    b. Name two isosceles triangles.   △EIU, △AOU
    c. Name four scalene triangles.
       △AIO, △EOI, △AEI, △AEO

Classify the triangles having sides as indicated.

4. 9, 2, 8   5. 5, 6, 5   6. 4.5, 4.5, 4.5   7. 7, 6.9, .7
scalene   isosceles   equilateral   scalene

Classifying Triangles by Angles ⑱

Acute △ — 3 acute angles
Obtuse △ — 1 obtuse angle
Right △ — 1 right angle
Equiangular △ — All angles ≅.

1. right   2. obtuse   3. obtuse   4. acute
5. equiangular   6. acute   7. right   8. acute
9. obtuse   10. right   11. right   12. equiangular

True or False

13. All equilateral triangles are isosceles triangles. __T__
14. Some scalene triangles are isosceles triangles. __F__
15. A right triangle may be an isosceles triangle. __T__
16. Every equiangular triangle is an acute triangle. __T__
17. An obtuse triangle has two acute angles. __T__
18. Some acute triangles are equiangular. __T__
19. A right triangle is also an equiangular triangle. __F__
20. Some isosceles triangles are acute. __T__

Interior Angles of a Triangle ⑲

For any △: x + y + z = 180°

m∠1 = ___
m∠1 + 65° + 36° = 180°
m∠1 + 101° = 180°
m∠1 = 79°

1. a = __60°__   2. b = __48__   3. c = __118°__   4. d = __74°__
5. e = __25°__   6. f = __60°__   7. x = __80°__   8. a = __45°__

9. If m∠1 = 74 and m∠3 = 39, m∠2 = __67°__
10. If m∠1 = 65 and m∠2 = 86, m∠3 = __29°__

11. x = __30°__
12. a = __36°__   2a = __72°__
13. x = __15°__   2x = __30°__   4x = __60°__   6x = __90°__
14. a = __20°__   3a = __60°__

Exterior and Interior Angles of a Tri ⑳

For any △: x + y = z

m∠2 = ___
38 + 31 = m∠2
69° = m∠2

Find the measures of the angles indicated.

1. g = __153°__   2. h = __78°__   3. i = __121°__   4. j = __137°__
5. k = __54°__   6. l = __46°__   7. a = __120°__   8. x = __45°__
9. z = __30°__   10. x = __40°__   11. x = __50°__   12. a = __130°__

13. If m∠1 = 88 and m∠2 = 27, m∠3 = __115°__
14. If m∠1 = 93 and m∠3 = 121, m∠2 = __28°__
15. x = __41°__

0-7424-1777-8 Intro to Geometry

Answer Key

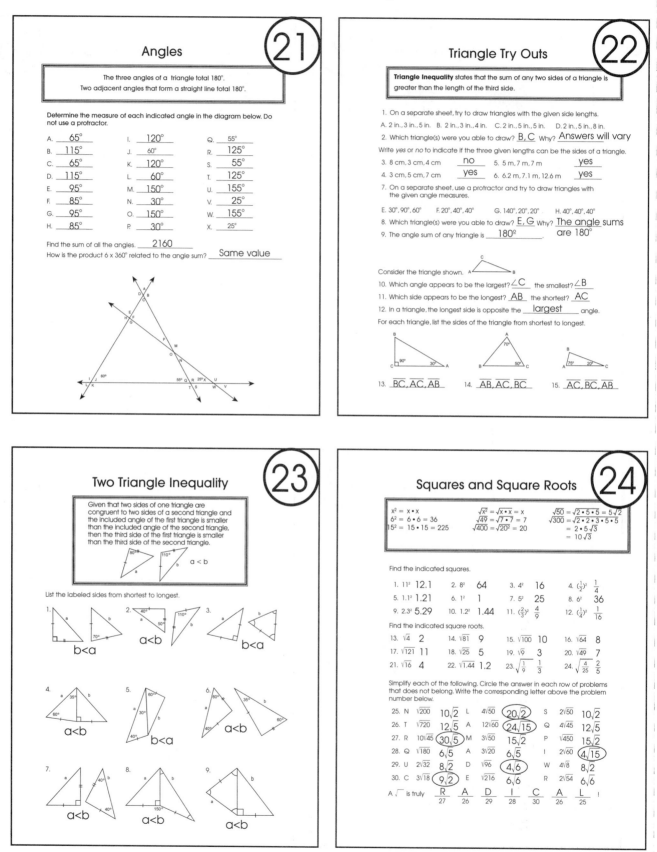

Angles ㉑

The three angles of a triangle total 180°.
Two adjacent angles that form a straight line total 180°.

Determine the measure of each indicated angle in the diagram below. Do not use a protractor.

A. 65°	I. 120°	Q. 55°
B. 115°	J. 60°	R. 125°
C. 65°	K. 120°	S. 55°
D. 115°	L. 60°	T. 125°
E. 95°	M. 150°	U. 155°
F. 85°	N. 30°	V. 25°
G. 95°	O. 150°	W. 155°
H. 85°	P. 30°	X. 25°

Find the sum of all the angles. __2160__
How is the product 6 x 360° related to the angle sum? __Same value__

Triangle Try Outs ㉒

Triangle Inequality states that the sum of any two sides of a triangle is greater than the length of the third side.

1. On a separate sheet, try to draw triangles with the given side lengths.
   A. 2 in., 3 in., 5 in.   B. 2 in., 3 in., 4 in.   C. 2 in., 5 in., 5 in.   D. 2 in., 5 in., 8 in.
2. Which triangle(s) were you able to draw? __B, C__ Why? __Answers will vary__

Write *yes* or *no* to indicate if the three given lengths can be the sides of a triangle.

3. 8 cm, 3 cm, 4 cm __no__   5. 5 m, 7 m, 7 m __yes__
4. 3 cm, 5 cm, 7 cm __yes__   6. 6.2 m, 7.1 m, 12.6 m __yes__

7. On a separate sheet, use a protractor and try to draw triangles with the given angle measures.
   E. 30°, 90°, 60°   F. 20°, 40°, 40°   G. 140°, 20°, 20°   H. 40°, 40°, 40°
8. Which triangle(s) were you able to draw? __E, G__ Why? __The angle sums are 180°__
9. The angle sum of any triangle is __180°__.

Consider the triangle shown.
10. Which angle appears to be the largest? __∠C__ the smallest? __∠B__
11. Which side appears to be the longest? __AB__ the shortest? __AC__
12. In a triangle, the longest side is opposite the __largest__ angle.

For each triangle, list the sides of the triangle from shortest to longest.

13. __BC, AC, AB__   14. __AB, AC, BC__   15. __AC, BC, AB__

Two Triangle Inequality ㉓

Given that two sides of one triangle are congruent to two sides of a second triangle and the included angle of the first triangle is smaller than the included angle of the second triangle, then the third side of the first triangle is smaller than the third side of the second triangle.

a < b

List the labeled sides from shortest to longest.

1. b<a   2. a<b   3. b<a
4. a<b   5. b<a   6. a<b
7. a<b   8. a<b   9. a<b

Squares and Square Roots ㉔

$$x^2 = x \cdot x$$
$$6^2 = 6 \cdot 6 = 36$$
$$15^2 = 15 \cdot 15 = 225$$

$$\sqrt{x^2} = \sqrt{x \cdot x} = x$$
$$\sqrt{49} = \sqrt{7 \cdot 7} = 7$$
$$\sqrt{400} = \sqrt{20^2} = 20$$

$$\sqrt{50} = \sqrt{2 \cdot 5 \cdot 5} = 5\sqrt{2}$$
$$\sqrt{300} = \sqrt{2 \cdot 2 \cdot 3 \cdot 5 \cdot 5}$$
$$= 2 \cdot 5\sqrt{3}$$
$$= 10\sqrt{3}$$

Find the indicated squares.

1. 11^2 12.1   2. 8^2 64   3. 4^2 16   4. $(\frac{1}{2})^2$ $\frac{1}{4}$
5. 1.1^2 1.21   6. 1^2 1   7. 5^2 25   8. 6^2 36
9. 2.3^2 5.29   10. 1.2^2 1.44   11. $(\frac{2}{3})^2$ $\frac{4}{9}$ 12. $(\frac{1}{4})^2$ $\frac{1}{16}$

Find the indicated square roots.

13. $\sqrt{4}$ 2   14. $\sqrt{81}$ 9   15. $\sqrt{100}$ 10   16. $\sqrt{64}$ 8
17. $\sqrt{121}$ 11   18. $\sqrt{25}$ 5   19. $\sqrt{9}$ 3   20. $\sqrt{49}$ 7
21. $\sqrt{16}$ 4   22. $\sqrt{1.44}$ 1.2   23. $\sqrt{\frac{1}{9}}$ $\frac{1}{3}$ 24. $\sqrt{\frac{4}{25}}$ $\frac{2}{5}$

Simplify each of the following. Circle the answer in each row of problems that does not belong. Write the corresponding letter above the problem number below.

25. N $\sqrt{200}$ $10\sqrt{2}$ L $4\sqrt{50}$ (20√2)   S $2\sqrt{50}$ $10\sqrt{2}$
26. T $\sqrt{720}$ $12\sqrt{5}$ A $12\sqrt{60}$ (24√15)   Q $4\sqrt{45}$ $12\sqrt{5}$
27. R $10\sqrt{45}$ (30√5)   M $3\sqrt{50}$ $15\sqrt{2}$ P $\sqrt{450}$ $15\sqrt{2}$
28. Q $\sqrt{180}$ $6\sqrt{5}$ A $3\sqrt{20}$ $6\sqrt{5}$ I $2\sqrt{60}$ (4√15)
29. U $2\sqrt{32}$ $8\sqrt{2}$ D $\sqrt{96}$ (4√6)   W $4\sqrt{8}$ $8\sqrt{2}$
30. C $3\sqrt{18}$ (9√2)   E $\sqrt{216}$ $6\sqrt{6}$ R $2\sqrt{54}$ $6\sqrt{6}$

A $\sqrt{\ }$ is truly __R A D I C A L__
      27 26 29 28 30 26 25

Answer Key

Right Triangles (25)

For any right Δ
$a^2 + b^2 = c^2$
(Pythagorean Theorem)

$3^2 + 4^2 = c^2$
$9 + 16 = c^2$
$25 = c^2$
$5 = c$

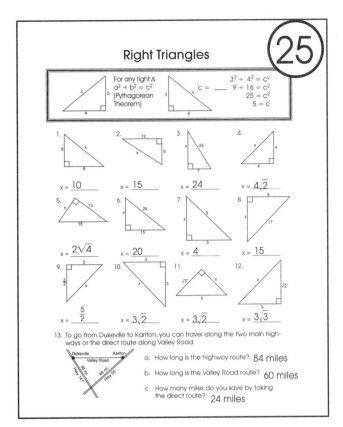

1. x = 10
2. x = 15
3. x = 24
4. x = $4\sqrt{2}$
5. x = $2\sqrt{4}$
6. x = 20
7. x = 4
8. x = 15
9. x = $\frac{5}{2}$
10. x = $3\sqrt{2}$
11. x = $3\sqrt{2}$
12. x = $3\sqrt{3}$

13. To go from Dukeville to Karlton, you can travel along the two main highways or the direct route along Valley Road.

a. How long is the highway route? **84 miles**
b. How long is the Valley Road route? **60 miles**
c. How many miles do you save by taking the direct route? **24 miles**

Special Right Triangles (26)

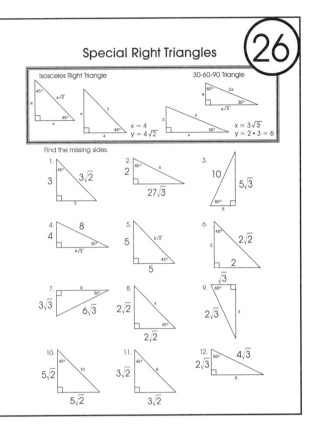

Isosceles Right Triangle

30-60-90 Triangle

x = 4
y = $4\sqrt{2}$

x = $3\sqrt{3}$
y = 2 • 3 = 6

Find the missing sides.

1. $3\sqrt{2}$
2. 2, $27\sqrt{3}$
3. $5\sqrt{3}$
4. 8
5. 5
6. $2\sqrt{2}$
7. $6\sqrt{3}$
8. $2\sqrt{2}$
9. $2\sqrt{3}$
10. $5\sqrt{2}$
11. $3\sqrt{2}$
12. $2\sqrt{3}$, $4\sqrt{3}$

Right Triangle Trigonometry (27)

sine	$\sin \theta = \frac{opposite}{hypotenuse}$	= $\frac{a}{c}$
cosine	$\cos \theta = \frac{adjacent}{hypotenuse}$	= $\frac{b}{c}$
tangent	$\tan \theta = \frac{opposite}{adjacent}$	= $\frac{a}{b}$
cosecant	$\csc \theta = \frac{1}{\sin \theta}$	= $\frac{c}{a}$
secant	$\sec \theta = \frac{1}{\cos \theta}$	= $\frac{c}{b}$
cotangent	$\cot \theta = \frac{1}{\tan \theta}$	= $\frac{b}{a}$

	sinθ	cosθ	tanθ	cscθ	secθ	cotθ
1.	4/5	3/5	4/3	5/4	5/3	3/4
2.	$\sqrt{2}/2$	$\sqrt{2}/2$	1	$\sqrt{2}$	$\sqrt{2}$	1
3.	1/2	$\sqrt{3}/2$	$\sqrt{3}/3$	2	$2\sqrt{3}/3$	$\sqrt{3}$
4.	4/5	3/5	4/3	5/4	5/3	3/4
5.	4/5	3/5	4/3	5/4	5/3	3/4
6.	5/13	12/13	5/12	13/5	13/12	12/5
7.	$\sqrt{2}/2$	$\sqrt{2}/2$	1	$\sqrt{2}$	$\sqrt{2}$	1
8.	15/17	8/17	15/8	17/15	17/8	8/15
9.	3/5	4/5	3/4	5/3	5/4	4/3
10.	15/17	8/17	15/8	17/15	17/8	8/15
11.	12/13	5/13	12/5	13/12	13/5	5/12
12.	$\sqrt{2}/2$	$\sqrt{2}/2$	1	$\sqrt{2}$	$\sqrt{2}$	1

Transformations (28)

Three Basic Movements
1. Translation (Slide)
2. Rotation (Turn)
3. Reflection (Flip)

Which single basic motion will make these figures coincide?

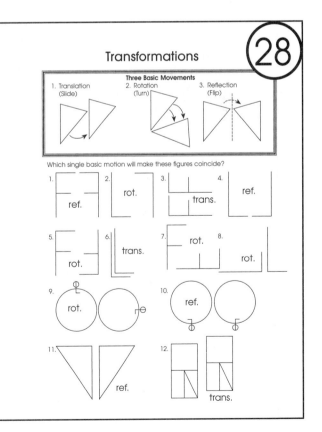

1. ref.
2. rot.
3. trans.
4. ref.
5. rot.
6. trans.
7. rot.
8. rot.
9. rot.
10. ref.
11. ref.
12. trans.

Answer Key

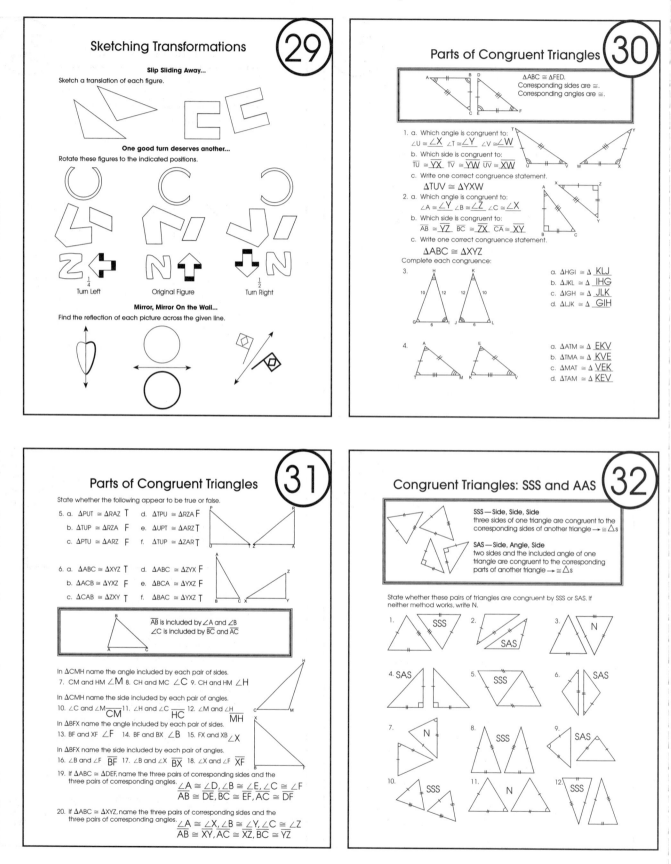

Sketching Transformations ㉙

Slip Sliding Away...

Sketch a translation of each figure.

One good turn deserves another...

Rotate these figures to the indicated positions.

Turn Left | Original Figure | Turn Right
$\frac{1}{4}$ | | $\frac{1}{2}$

Mirror, Mirror On the Wall...

Find the reflection of each picture across the given line.

Parts of Congruent Triangles ㉚

△ABC ≅ △FED.
Corresponding sides are ≅.
Corresponding angles are ≅.

1. a. Which angle is congruent to:
   ∠U ≅ ∠X   ∠T ≅ ∠Y   ∠V ≅ ∠W
   b. Which side is congruent to:
   $\overline{TU}$ ≅ $\overline{YX}$ $\overline{TV}$ ≅ $\overline{YW}$ $\overline{UV}$ ≅ $\overline{XW}$
   c. Write one correct congruence statement.
   △TUV ≅ △YXW

2. a. Which angle is congruent to:
   ∠A ≅ ∠Y   ∠B ≅ ∠Z   ∠C ≅ ∠X
   b. Which side is congruent to:
   $\overline{AB}$ ≅ $\overline{YZ}$ $\overline{BC}$ ≅ $\overline{ZX}$ $\overline{CA}$ ≅ $\overline{XY}$
   c. Write one correct congruence statement.
   △ABC ≅ △XYZ

Complete each congruence:

3.
   a. △HGI ≅ △ KLJ
   b. △JKL ≅ △ IHG
   c. △IGH ≅ △ JLK
   d. △LJK ≅ △ GIH

4.
   a. △ATM ≅ △ EKV
   b. △TMA ≅ △ KVE
   c. △MAT ≅ △ VEK
   d. △TAM ≅ △ KEV

Parts of Congruent Triangles ㉛

State whether the following appear to be true or false.

5. a. △PUT ≅ △RAZ T   d. △TPU ≅ △RZA F
   b. △TUP ≅ △RZA F   e. △UPT ≅ △ARZ T
   c. △PTU ≅ △ARZ F   f. △TUP ≅ △ZAR T

6. a. △ABC ≅ △XYZ T   d. △ABC ≅ △ZYX F
   b. △ACB ≅ △YXZ F   e. △BCA ≅ △YXZ F
   c. △CAB ≅ △ZXY T   f. △BAC ≅ △YXZ T

$\overline{AB}$ is included by ∠A and ∠B
∠C is included by $\overline{BC}$ and $\overline{AC}$

In △CMH name the angle included by each pair of sides.
7. CM and HM ∠M   8. CH and MC ∠C   9. CH and HM ∠H

In △CMH name the side included by each pair of angles.
10. ∠C and ∠M $\overline{CM}$ 11. ∠H and ∠C $\overline{HC}$ 12. ∠M and ∠H $\overline{MH}$

In △BFX name the angle included by each pair of sides.
13. BF and XF ∠F   14. BF and BX ∠B   15. FX and XB ∠X

In △BFX name the side included by each pair of angles.
16. ∠B and ∠F $\overline{BF}$ 17. ∠B and ∠X $\overline{BX}$ 18. ∠X and ∠F $\overline{XF}$

19. If △ABC ≅ △DEF, name the three pairs of corresponding sides and the three pairs of corresponding angles.
    ∠A ≅ ∠D, ∠B ≅ ∠E, ∠C ≅ ∠F
    $\overline{AB}$ ≅ $\overline{DE}$, BC ≅ $\overline{EF}$, AC ≅ $\overline{DF}$

20. If △ABC ≅ △XYZ, name the three pairs of corresponding sides and the three pairs of corresponding angles.
    ∠A ≅ ∠X, ∠B ≅ ∠Y, ∠C ≅ ∠Z
    $\overline{AB}$ ≅ $\overline{XY}$, AC ≅ $\overline{XZ}$, BC ≅ $\overline{YZ}$

Congruent Triangles: SSS and AAS ㉜

SSS — Side, Side, Side
three sides of one triangle are congruent to the corresponding sides of another triangle → ≅ △s

SAS — Side, Angle, Side
two sides and the included angle of one triangle are congruent to the corresponding parts of another triangle → ≅ △s

State whether these pairs of triangles are congruent by SSS or SAS. If neither method works, write N.

1. SSS   2. SAS   3. N
4. SAS   5. SSS   6. SAS
7. N   8. SSS   9. SAS
10. SSS   11. N   12. SSS

Answer Key

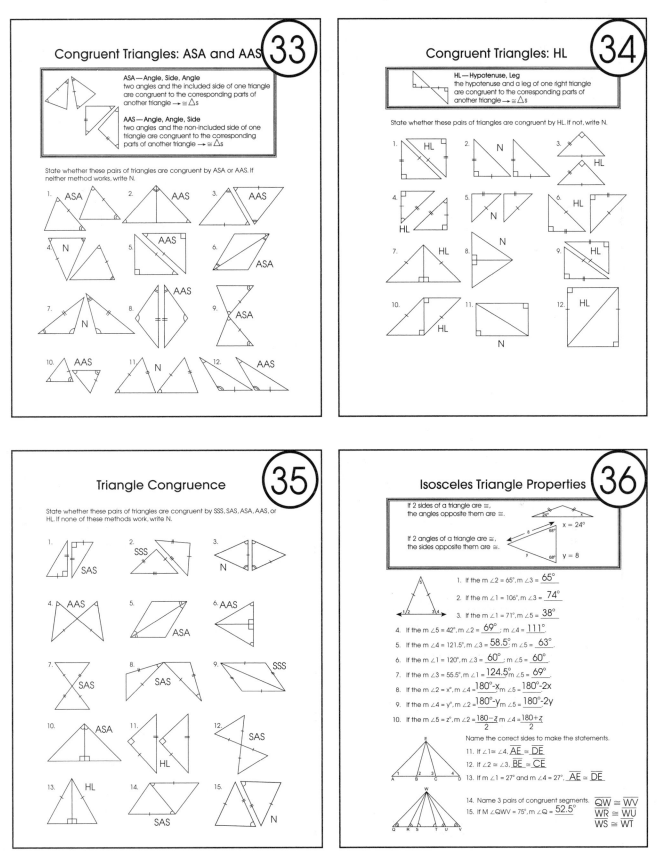

Congruent Triangles: ASA and AAS (33)

ASA—Angle, Side, Angle
two angles and the included side of one triangle
are congruent to the corresponding parts of
another triangle → ≅ △s

AAS—Angle, Angle, Side
two angles and the non-included side of one
triangle are congruent to the corresponding
parts of another triangle → ≅ △s

State whether these pairs of triangles are congruent by ASA or AAS. If
neither method works, write N.

1. ASA
2. AAS
3. AAS
4. N
5. AAS
6. ASA
7. N
8. AAS
9. ASA
10. AAS
11. N
12. AAS

Congruent Triangles: HL (34)

HL—Hypotenuse, Leg
the hypotenuse and a leg of one right triangle
are congruent to the corresponding parts of
another triangle → ≅ △s

State whether these pairs of triangles are congruent by HL. If not, write N.

1. HL
2. N
3. HL
4. HL
5. N
6. HL
7. HL
8. N
9. HL
10. HL
11. N
12. HL

Triangle Congruence (35)

State whether these pairs of triangles are congruent by SSS, SAS, ASA, AAS, or
HL. If none of these methods work, write N.

1. SAS
2. SSS
3. N
4. AAS
5. ASA
6. AAS
7. SAS
8. SAS
9. SSS
10. ASA
11. HL
12. SAS
13. HL
14. SAS
15. N

Isosceles Triangle Properties (36)

If 2 sides of a triangle are ≅,
the angles opposite them are ≅.

If 2 angles of a triangle are ≅,
the sides opposite them are ≅.

x = 24°

y = 8

1. If the m ∠2 = 65°, m ∠3 = $65°$
2. If the m ∠1 = 106°, m ∠3 = $74°$
3. If the m ∠1 = 71°, m ∠5 = $38°$
4. If the m ∠5 = 42°, m ∠2 = $69°$; m ∠4 = $111°$
5. If the m ∠4 = 121.5°, m ∠3 = $58.5°$; m ∠5 = $63°$
6. If the m ∠1 = 120°, m ∠3 = $60°$; m ∠5 = $60°$
7. If the m ∠3 = 55.5°, m ∠1 = $124.5°$ m ∠5 = $69°$.
8. If the m ∠2 = x°, m ∠4 = $180°-x$ m ∠5 = $180°-2x$
9. If the m ∠4 = y°, m ∠2 = $180°-y$ m ∠5 = $180°-2y$
10. If the m ∠5 = z°, m ∠2 = $\frac{180-z}{2}$ m ∠4 = $\frac{180+z}{2}$

Name the correct sides to make the statements.

11. If ∠1 ≅ ∠4, $\overline{AE} ≅ \overline{DE}$
12. If ∠2 ≅ ∠3, $\overline{BE} ≅ \overline{CE}$
13. If m ∠1 = 27° and m ∠4 = 27°, $\overline{AE} ≅ \overline{DE}$

14. Name 3 pairs of congruent segments. $\overline{QW} ≅ \overline{WV}$
    $\overline{WR} ≅ \overline{WU}$
15. If M ∠QWV = 75°, m ∠Q = $52.5°$ $\overline{WS} ≅ \overline{WT}$

Answer Key

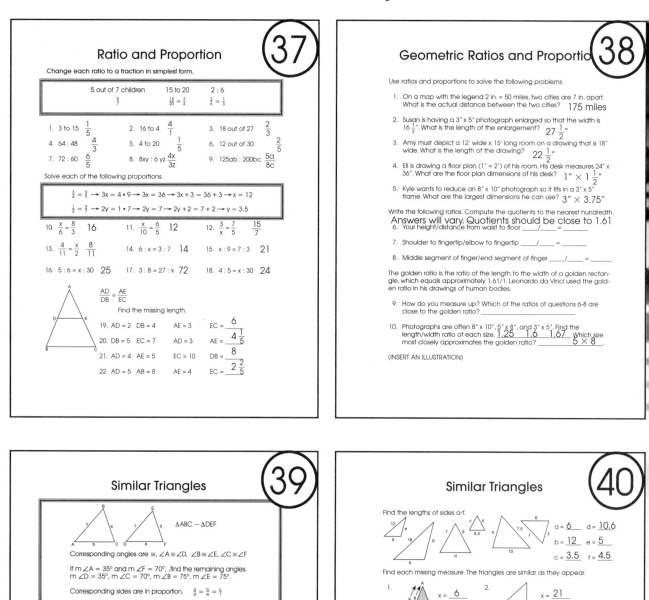

Ratio and Proportion (37)

Change each ratio to a fraction in simplest form.

5 out of 7 children	15 to 20	2 : 6
$\frac{5}{7}$	$\frac{15}{20} = \frac{3}{4}$	$\frac{2}{6} = \frac{1}{3}$

1. 3 to 15 $\frac{1}{5}$
2. 16 to 4 $\frac{4}{1}$
3. 18 out of 27 $\frac{2}{3}$
4. 64 : 48 $\frac{4}{3}$
5. 4 to 20 $\frac{1}{5}$
6. 12 out of 30 $\frac{2}{5}$
7. 72 : 60 $\frac{6}{5}$
8. 8xy : 6 yz $\frac{4x}{3z}$
9. 125ab : 200bc $\frac{5a}{8c}$

Solve each of the following proportions.

$\frac{3}{4} = \frac{9}{x} \rightarrow 3x = 4 \cdot 9 \rightarrow 3x = 36 \rightarrow 3x \div 3 = 36 \div 3 \rightarrow x = 12$

$\frac{1}{2} = \frac{y}{7} \rightarrow 2y = 1 \cdot 7 \rightarrow 2y = 7 \rightarrow 2y \div 2 = 7 \div 2 \rightarrow y = 3.5$

10. $\frac{x}{6} = \frac{8}{3}$ 16
11. $\frac{x}{10} = \frac{6}{5}$ 12
12. $\frac{3}{x} = \frac{7}{5}$ $\frac{15}{7}$

13. $\frac{4}{11} = \frac{x}{2}$ $\frac{8}{11}$
14. 6 : x = 3 : 7   14
15. x : 9 = 7 : 3   21

16. 5 : 6 = x : 30   25
17. 3 : 8 = 27 : x   72
18. 4 : 5 = x : 30   24

$\frac{AD}{DB} = \frac{AE}{EC}$

Find the missing length.

19. AD = 2   DB = 4   AE = 3   EC = 6

20. DB = 5   EC = 7   AD = 3   AE = $4\frac{1}{5}$

21. AD = 4   AE = 5   EC = 10   DB = 8

22. AD = 5   AB = 8   AE = 4   EC = $2\frac{2}{5}$

Geometric Ratios and Proportions (38)

Use ratios and proportions to solve the following problems.

1. On a map with the legend 2 in. = 50 miles, two cities are 7 in. apart. What is the actual distance between the two cities?   175 miles

2. Susan is having a 3" x 5" photograph enlarged so that the width is $16\frac{1}{2}$". What is the length of the enlargement? $27\frac{1}{2}$"

3. Amy must depict a 12' wide x 15' long room on a drawing that is 18" wide. What is the length of the drawing? $22\frac{1}{2}$"

4. Eli is drawing a floor plan (1" = 2') of his room. His desk measures 24" x 36". What are the floor plan dimensions of his desk? $1'' \times 1\frac{1}{2}''$

5. Kyle wants to reduce an 8" x 10" photograph so it fits in a 3" x 5" frame. What are the largest dimensions he can use? $3'' \times 3.75''$

Write the following ratios. Compute the quotients to the nearest hundredth.
Answers will vary. Quotients should be close to 1.61

6. Your height/distance from waist to floor ____/____ = _____

7. Shoulder to fingertip/elbow to fingertip ____/____ = _____

8. Middle segment of finger/end segment of finger ____/____ = _____

The golden ratio is the ratio of the length to the width of a golden rectangle, which equals approximately 1.61/1. Leonardo da Vinci used the golden ratio in his drawings of human bodies.

9. How do you measure up? Which of the ratios of questions 6-8 are close to the golden ratio? _____

10. Photographs are often 8" x 10", 5" x 8", and 3" x 5". Find the length/width ratio of each size. 1.25   1.6   1.67 Which size most closely approximates the golden ratio? 5×8.

(INSERT AN ILLUSTRATION)

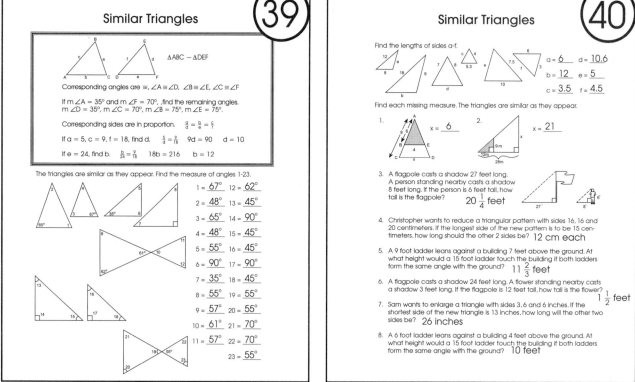

Similar Triangles (39)

ΔABC ~ ΔDEF

Corresponding angles are ≅, ∠A ≅ ∠D, ∠B ≅ ∠E, ∠C ≅ ∠F

If m∠A = 35° and m∠F = 70°, find the remaining angles.
m∠D = 35°, m∠C = 70°, m∠B = 75°, m∠E = 75°.

Corresponding sides are in proportion. $\frac{a}{d} = \frac{b}{e} = \frac{c}{f}$

If a = 5, c = 9, f = 18, find d. $\frac{5}{d} = \frac{9}{18}$ 9d = 90   d = 10

If e = 24, find b. $\frac{b}{24} = \frac{9}{18}$ 18b = 216   b = 12

The triangles are similar as they appear. Find the measure of angles 1-23.

1 = 67°
2 = 48°
3 = 65°
4 = 48°
5 = 55°
6 = 90°
7 = 35°
8 = 55°
9 = 57°
10 = 61°
11 = 57°
12 = 62°
13 = 45°
14 = 90°
15 = 45°
16 = 45°
17 = 90°
18 = 45°
19 = 55°
20 = 55°
21 = 70°
22 = 70°
23 = 55°

Similar Triangles (40)

Find the lengths of sides a-f.

a = 6   d = 10.6
b = 12   e = 5
c = 3.5   f = 4.5

Find each missing measure. The triangles are similar as they appear.

1. x = 6
2. x = 21

3. A flagpole casts a shadow 27 feet long. A person standing nearby casts a shadow 8 feet long. If the person is 6 feet tall, how tall is the flagpole? $20\frac{1}{4}$ feet

4. Christopher wants to reduce a triangular pattern with sides 16, 16 and 20 centimeters. If the longest side of the new pattern is to be 15 centimeters, how long should the other 2 sides be?   12 cm each

5. A 9 foot ladder leans against a building 7 feet above the ground. At what height would a 15 foot ladder touch the building if both ladders form the same angle with the ground? $11\frac{2}{3}$ feet

6. A flagpole casts a shadow 24 feet long. A flower standing nearby casts a shadow 3 feet long. If the flagpole is 12 feet tall, how tall is the flower? $1\frac{1}{2}$ feet

7. Sam wants to enlarge a triangle with sides 3, 6 and 6 inches. If the shortest side of the new triangle is 13 inches, how long will the other two sides be?   26 inches

8. A 6 foot ladder leans against a building 4 feet above the ground. At what height would a 15 foot ladder touch the building if both ladders form the same angle with the ground?   10 feet

0-7424-1777-8 *Intro to Geometry*

Answer Key

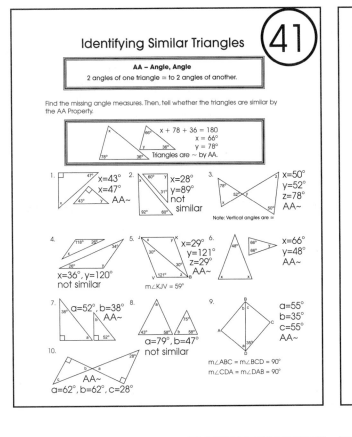

Identifying Similar Triangles (41)

AA – Angle, Angle
2 angles of one triangle ≅ to 2 angles of another.

Find the missing angle measures. Then, tell whether the triangles are similar by the AA Property.

$$x + 78 + 36 = 180$$
$$x = 66°$$
$$y = 78°$$
Triangles are ~ by AA.

1. x=43°, x=47°, AA~
2. x=28°, y=89°, not similar
3. x=50°, y=52°, z=78°, AA~ Note: Vertical angles are ≅
4. x=36°, y=120°, not similar
5. x=29°, y=121°, z=29°, AA~ m∠KJV = 59°
6. x=66°, y=48°, AA~
7. a=52°, b=38°, AA~
8. a=79°, b=47°, not similar
9. a=55°, b=35°, c=55°, AA~
10. AA~, a=62°, b=62°, c=28° m∠ABC = m∠BCD = 90° m∠CDA = m∠DAB = 90°

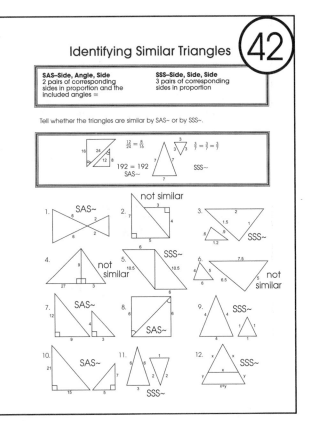

Identifying Similar Triangles (42)

SAS–Side, Angle, Side
2 pairs of corresponding sides in proportion and the included angles ≅

SSS–Side, Side, Side
3 pairs of corresponding sides in proportion

Tell whether the triangles are similar by SAS~ or by SSS~.

$$\frac{12}{24} = \frac{8}{16} \qquad \frac{3}{3} = \frac{3}{7} = \frac{3}{7}$$
$$192 = 192$$
SAS~ SSS~

1. SAS~
2. not similar
3. SSS~
4. not similar
5. SSS~
6. not similar
7. SAS~
8. SAS~
9. SSS~
10. SAS~
11. SSS~
12. SSS~

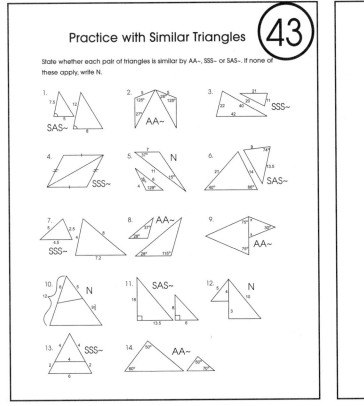

Practice with Similar Triangles (43)

State whether each pair of triangles is similar by AA~, SSS~ or SAS~. If none of these apply, write N.

1. SAS~
2. AA~
3. SSS~
4. SSS~
5. N
6. SAS~
7. SSS~
8. AA~
9. AA~
10. N
11. SAS~
12. N
13. SSS~
14. AA~

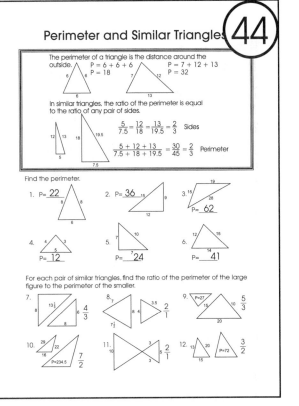

Perimeter and Similar Triangles (44)

The perimeter of a triangle is the distance around the outside.
$$P = 6 + 6 + 6 \qquad P = 7 + 12 + 13$$
$$P = 18 \qquad P = 32$$

In similar triangles, the ratio of the perimeter is equal to the ratio of any pair of sides.
$$\frac{5}{7.5} = \frac{12}{18} = \frac{13}{19.5} = \frac{2}{3} \quad \text{Sides}$$
$$\frac{5 + 12 + 13}{7.5 + 18 + 19.5} = \frac{30}{45} = \frac{2}{3} \quad \text{Perimeter}$$

Find the perimeter.

1. P= 22
2. P= 36
3. P= 62
4. P= 12
5. P= 24
6. P= 41

For each pair of similar triangles, find the ratio of the perimeter of the large figure to the perimeter of the smaller.

7. $\frac{4}{3}$
8. $\frac{2}{1}$
9. $\frac{5}{3}$
10. $\frac{7}{2}$
11. $\frac{2}{1}$
12. $\frac{3}{2}$

Answer Key

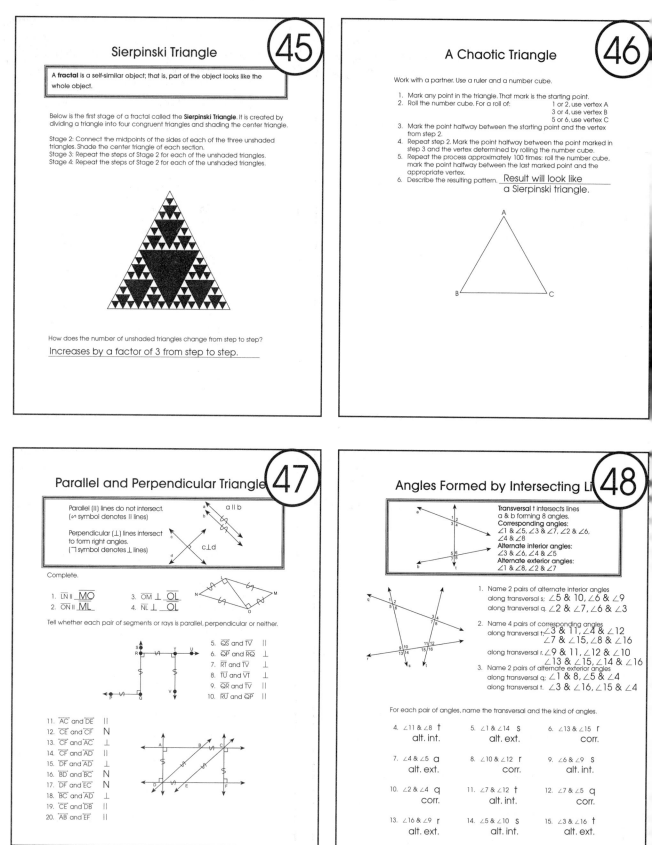

45 Sierpinski Triangle

A **fractal** is a self-similar object; that is, part of the object looks like the whole object.

Below is the first stage of a fractal called the **Sierpinski Triangle**. It is created by dividing a triangle into four congruent triangles and shading the center triangle.

Stage 2: Connect the midpoints of the sides of each of the three unshaded triangles. Shade the center triangle of each section.
Stage 3: Repeat the steps of Stage 2 for each of the unshaded triangles.
Stage 4: Repeat the steps of Stage 2 for each of the unshaded triangles.

How does the number of unshaded triangles change from step to step?

Increases by a factor of 3 from step to step.

46 A Chaotic Triangle

Work with a partner. Use a ruler and a number cube.

1. Mark any point in the triangle. That mark is the starting point.
2. Roll the number cube. For a roll of:
   1 or 2, use vertex A
   3 or 4, use vertex B
   5 or 6, use vertex C
3. Mark the point halfway between the starting point and the vertex from step 2.
4. Repeat step 2. Mark the point halfway between the point marked in step 3 and the vertex determined by rolling the number cube.
5. Repeat the process approximately 100 times: roll the number cube, mark the point halfway between the last marked point and the appropriate vertex.
6. Describe the resulting pattern. Result will look like a Sierpinski triangle.

47 Parallel and Perpendicular Triangle

Parallel (II) lines do not intersect.
(⋌ symbol denotes II lines)

Perpendicular (⊥) lines intersect to form right angles.
(⌐ symbol denotes ⊥ lines)

a II b

c ⊥ d

Complete.

1. $\overline{LN}$ II MO
2. $\overline{ON}$ II ML
3. $\overline{OM}$ ⊥ OL
4. $\overline{NL}$ ⊥ OL

Tell whether each pair of segments or rays is parallel, perpendicular or neither.

5. $\overline{QS}$ and $\overline{TV}$ II
6. $\overline{QP}$ and $\overline{RQ}$ ⊥
7. $\overline{RT}$ and $\overline{TV}$ ⊥
8. $\overline{TU}$ and $\overline{VT}$ ⊥
9. $\overline{QR}$ and $\overline{TV}$ II
10. $\overline{RU}$ and $\overline{QP}$ II

11. $\overline{AC}$ and $\overline{DE}$ II
12. $\overline{CE}$ and $\overline{CF}$ N
13. $\overline{CF}$ and $\overline{AC}$ ⊥
14. $\overline{CF}$ and $\overline{AD}$ II
15. $\overline{DF}$ and $\overline{AD}$ ⊥
16. $\overline{BD}$ and $\overline{BC}$ N
17. $\overline{DF}$ and $\overline{EC}$ N
18. $\overline{BC}$ and $\overline{AD}$ ⊥
19. $\overline{CE}$ and $\overline{DB}$ II
20. $\overline{AB}$ and $\overline{EF}$ II

48 Angles Formed by Intersecting Lines

Transversal t intersects lines a & b forming 8 angles.
Corresponding angles:
∠1 & ∠5, ∠3 & ∠7, ∠2 & ∠6, ∠4 & ∠8
Alternate interior angles:
∠3 & ∠6, ∠4 & ∠5
Alternate exterior angles:
∠1 & ∠8, ∠2 & ∠7

1. Name 2 pairs of alternate interior angles
   along transversal s; ∠5 & ∠10, ∠6 & ∠9
   along transversal q. ∠2 & ∠7, ∠6 & ∠3

2. Name 4 pairs of corresponding angles
   along transversal t; ∠3 & ∠11, ∠4 & ∠12
   ∠7 & ∠15, ∠8 & ∠16
   along transversal r. ∠9 & ∠11, ∠12 & ∠10
   ∠13 & ∠15, ∠14 & ∠16

3. Name 2 pairs of alternate exterior angles
   along transversal q; ∠1 & ∠8, ∠5 & ∠4
   along transversal t. ∠3 & ∠16, ∠15 & ∠4

For each pair of angles, name the transversal and the kind of angles.

4. ∠11 & ∠8 t
   alt. int.
5. ∠1 & ∠14 S
   alt. ext.
6. ∠13 & ∠15 r
   corr.

7. ∠4 & ∠5 a
   alt. ext.
8. ∠10 & ∠12 r
   corr.
9. ∠6 & ∠9 S
   alt. int.

10. ∠2 & ∠4 q
    corr.
11. ∠7 & ∠12 t
    alt. int.
12. ∠7 & ∠5 q
    corr.

13. ∠16 & ∠9 r
    alt. ext.
14. ∠5 & ∠10 S
    alt. int.
15. ∠3 & ∠16 t
    alt. ext.

0-7424-1777-8 *Intro to Geometry*

Answer Key

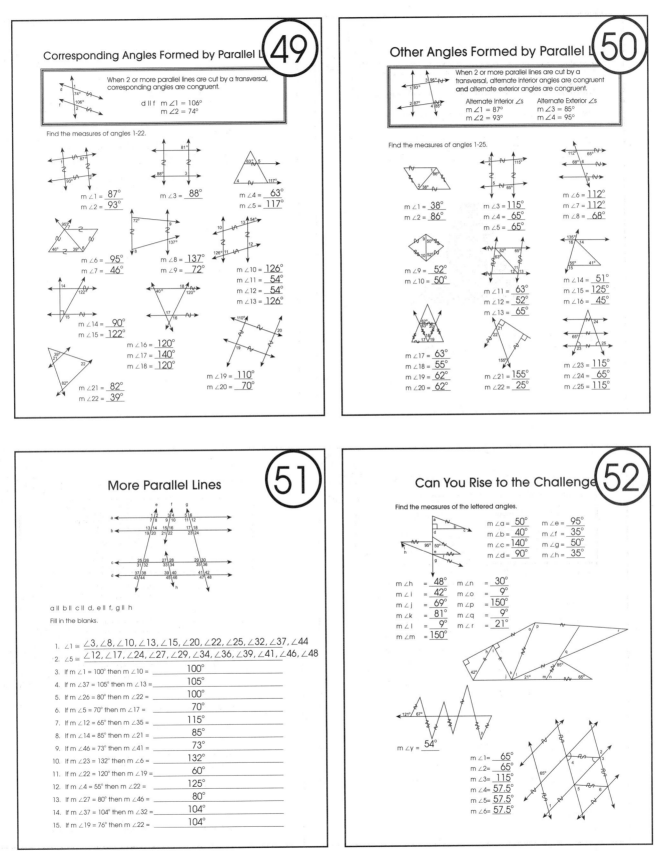

Corresponding Angles Formed by Parallel L ④⑨

When 2 or more parallel lines are cut by a transversal, corresponding angles are congruent.

d ‖ f   m ∠1 = 106°
m ∠2 = 74°

Find the measures of angles 1-22.

m ∠1 = __87°__
m ∠2 = __93°__

m ∠3 = __88°__

m ∠4 = __63°__
m ∠5 = __117°__

m ∠6 = __95°__
m ∠7 = __46°__

m ∠8 = __137°__
m ∠9 = __72°__

m ∠10 = __126°__
m ∠11 = __54°__
m ∠12 = __54°__
m ∠13 = __126°__

m ∠14 = __90°__
m ∠15 = __122°__

m ∠16 = __120°__
m ∠17 = __140°__
m ∠18 = __120°__

m ∠19 = __110°__
m ∠20 = __70°__

m ∠21 = __82°__
m ∠22 = __39°__

Other Angles Formed by Parallel L ⑤⓪

When 2 or more parallel lines are cut by a transversal, alternate interior angles are congruent and alternate exterior angles are congruent.

Alternate Interior ∠s	Alternate Exterior ∠s
m ∠1 = 87°	m ∠3 = 85°
m ∠2 = 93°	m ∠4 = 95°

Find the measures of angles 1-25.

m ∠1 = __38°__
m ∠2 = __86°__

m ∠3 = __115°__
m ∠4 = __65°__
m ∠5 = __65°__

m ∠6 = __112°__
m ∠7 = __112°__
m ∠8 = __68°__

m ∠9 = __52°__
m ∠10 = __50°__

m ∠11 = __63°__
m ∠12 = __52°__
m ∠13 = __65°__

m ∠14 = __51°__
m ∠15 = __125°__
m ∠16 = __45°__

m ∠17 = __63°__
m ∠18 = __55°__
m ∠19 = __62°__
m ∠20 = __62°__

m ∠21 = __155°__
m ∠22 = __25°__

m ∠23 = __115°__
m ∠24 = __65°__
m ∠25 = __115°__

More Parallel Lines ⑤①

a ‖ b ‖ c ‖ d, e ‖ f, g ‖ h

Fill in the blanks.

1. ∠1 ≅ __∠3, ∠8, ∠10, ∠13, ∠15, ∠20, ∠22, ∠25, ∠32, ∠37, ∠44__
2. ∠5 ≅ __∠12, ∠17, ∠24, ∠27, ∠29, ∠34, ∠36, ∠39, ∠41, ∠46, ∠48__
3. If m ∠1 = 100° then m ∠10 = __100°__
4. If m ∠37 = 105° then m ∠13 = __105°__
5. If m ∠26 = 80° then m ∠22 = __100°__
6. If m ∠5 = 70° then m ∠17 = __70°__
7. If m ∠12 = 65° then m ∠35 = __115°__
8. If m ∠14 = 85° then m ∠21 = __85°__
9. If m ∠46 = 73° then m ∠41 = __73°__
10. If m ∠23 = 132° then m ∠6 = __132°__
11. If m ∠22 = 120° then m ∠19 = __60°__
12. If m ∠4 = 55° then m ∠22 = __125°__
13. If m ∠27 = 80° then m ∠46 = __80°__
14. If m ∠37 = 104° then m ∠32 = __104°__
15. If m ∠19 = 76° then m ∠22 = __104°__

Can You Rise to the Challenge ⑤②

Find the measures of the lettered angles.

m ∠a = __50°__   m ∠e = __95°__
m ∠b = __40°__   m ∠f = __35°__
m ∠c = __140°__   m ∠g = __50°__
m ∠d = __90°__   m ∠h = __35°__

m ∠h = __48°__   m ∠n = __30°__
m ∠i = __42°__   m ∠o = __9°__
m ∠j = __69°__   m ∠p = __150°__
m ∠k = __81°__   m ∠q = __9°__
m ∠l = __9°__   m ∠r = __21°__
m ∠m = __150°__

m ∠y = __54°__

m ∠1 = __65°__
m ∠2 = __65°__
m ∠3 = __115°__
m ∠4 = __57.5°__
m ∠5 = __57.5°__
m ∠6 = __57.5°__

Answer Key

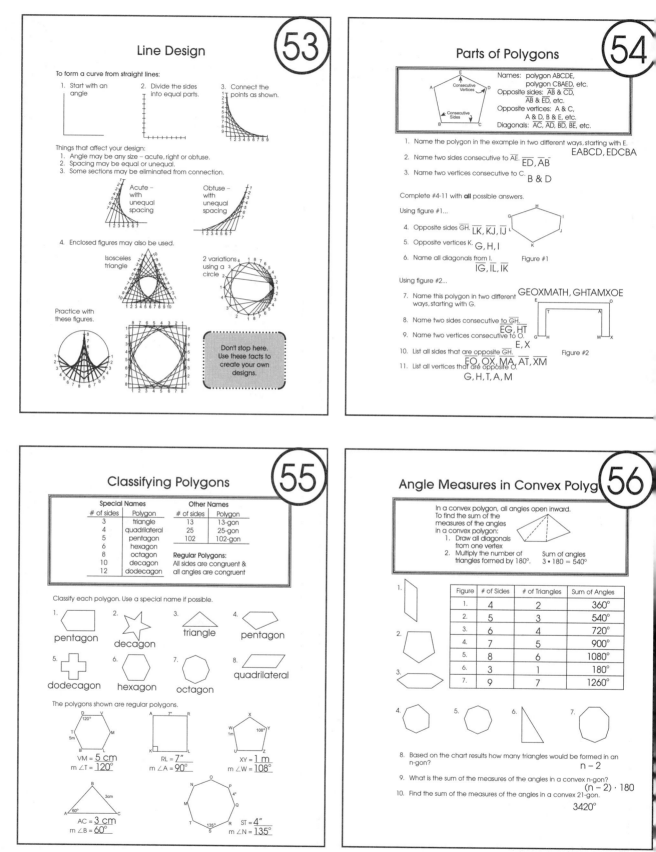

Line Design (53)

To form a curve from straight lines:

1. Start with an angle
2. Divide the sides into equal parts.
3. Connect the points as shown.

Things that affect your design:
1. Angle may be any size – acute, right or obtuse.
2. Spacing may be equal or unequal.
3. Some sections may be eliminated from connection.

Acute – with unequal spacing

Obtuse – with unequal spacing

4. Enclosed figures may also be used.

Isosceles triangle

2 variations using a circle

Practice with these figures.

Don't stop here. Use these facts to create your own designs.

Parts of Polygons (54)

Names: polygon ABCDE, polygon CBAED, etc.
Opposite sides: $\overline{AB}$ & $\overline{CD}$, $\overline{AB}$ & $\overline{ED}$, etc.
Opposite vertices: A & C, A & D, B & E, etc.
Diagonals: $\overline{AC}$, $\overline{AD}$, $\overline{BD}$, $\overline{BE}$, etc.

1. Name the polygon in the example in two different ways, starting with E. **EABCD, EDCBA**
2. Name two sides consecutive to $\overline{AE}$. **$\overline{ED}$, $\overline{AB}$**
3. Name two vertices consecutive to C. **B & D**

Complete #4-11 with **all** possible answers.

Using figure #1...

4. Opposite sides $\overline{GH}$. **$\overline{LK}$, $\overline{KJ}$, $\overline{IJ}$**
5. Opposite vertices K. **G, H, I**
6. Name all diagonals from I. **$\overline{IG}$, $\overline{IL}$, $\overline{IK}$**

Figure #1

Using figure #2...

7. Name this polygon in two different ways, starting with G. **GEOXMATH, GHTAMXOE**
8. Name two sides consecutive to $\overline{GH}$. **$\overline{EG}$, $\overline{HT}$**
9. Name two vertices consecutive to O. **E, X**
10. List all sides that are opposite $\overline{GH}$. **$\overline{EO}$, $\overline{OX}$, $\overline{MA}$, $\overline{AT}$, $\overline{XM}$**
11. List all vertices that are opposite O. **G, H, T, A, M**

Figure #2

Classifying Polygons (55)

Special Names		Other Names	
# of sides	Polygon	# of sides	Polygon
3	triangle	13	13-gon
4	quadrilateral	25	25-gon
5	pentagon	102	102-gon
6	hexagon		
8	octagon	**Regular Polygons:**	
10	decagon	All sides are congruent &	
12	dodecagon	all angles are congruent	

Classify each polygon. Use a special name if possible.

1. pentagon
2. decagon
3. triangle
4. pentagon
5. dodecagon
6. hexagon
7. octagon
8. quadrilateral

The polygons shown are regular polygons.

VM = **5 cm**
m ∠T = **120°**

RL = **7"**
m ∠A = **90°**

XY = **1 m**
m ∠W = **108°**

AC = **3 cm**
m ∠B = **60°**

ST = **4"**
m ∠N = **135°**

Angle Measures in Convex Polygons (56)

In a convex polygon, all angles open inward. To find the sum of the measures of the angles in a convex polygon:
1. Draw all diagonals from one vertex
2. Multiply the number of triangles formed by 180°.

Sum of angles
$3 \cdot 180 = 540°$

Figure	# of Sides	# of Triangles	Sum of Angles
1.	4	2	360°
2.	5	3	540°
3.	6	4	720°
4.	7	5	900°
5.	8	6	1080°
6.	3	1	180°
7.	9	7	1260°

8. Based on the chart results how many triangles would be formed in an n-gon? **n − 2**
9. What is the sum of the measures of the angles in a convex n-gon? **$(n − 2) \cdot 180$**
10. Find the sum of the measures of the angles in a convex 21-gon. **3420°**

Answer Key

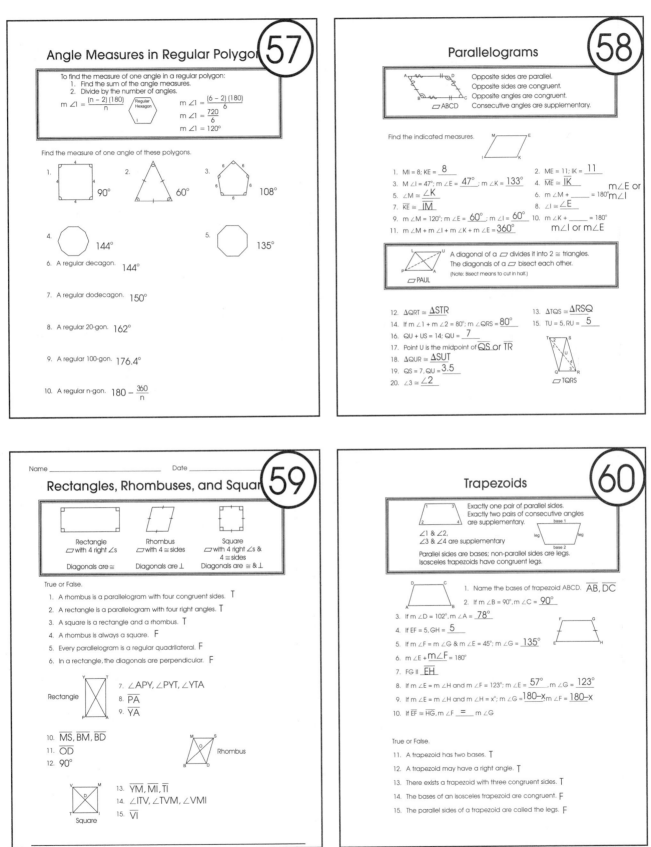

57 — Angle Measures in Regular Polygons

To find the measure of one angle in a regular polygon:
1. Find the sum of the angle measures.
2. Divide by the number of angles.

$$m \angle 1 = \frac{(n-2)(180)}{n}$$

Regular Hexagon

$$m \angle 1 = \frac{(6-2)(180)}{6}$$
$$m \angle 1 = \frac{720}{6}$$
$$m \angle 1 = 120°$$

Find the measure of one angle of these polygons.

1. 90°
2. 60°
3. 108°
4. 144°
5. 135°
6. A regular decagon. 144°
7. A regular dodecagon. 150°
8. A regular 20-gon. 162°
9. A regular 100-gon. 176.4°
10. A regular n-gon. $180 - \frac{360}{n}$

58 — Parallelograms

Opposite sides are parallel.
Opposite sides are congruent.
Opposite angles are congruent.
Consecutive angles are supplementary.

▱ABCD

Find the indicated measures.

1. MI = 8; KE = __8__
2. ME = 11; IK = __11__
3. m ∠I = 47°; m ∠E = __47°__ ; m ∠K = __133°__
4. $\overline{ME} \cong$ __IK__
5. ∠M ≅ __∠K__
6. m ∠M + ____ = 180° m∠E or m∠I
7. $\overline{KE} \cong$ __IM__
8. ∠I ≅ __∠E__
9. m ∠M = 120°; m ∠E = __60°__ ; m ∠I = __60°__
10. m ∠K + ____ = 180° m∠I or m∠E
11. m ∠M + m ∠I + m ∠K + m ∠E = __360°__

A diagonal of a ▱ divides it into 2 ≅ triangles.
The diagonals of a ▱ bisect each other.
(Note: Bisect means to cut in half.)

▱PAUL

12. △QRT ≅ __△STR__
13. △TQS ≅ __△RSQ__
14. If m ∠1 + m ∠2 = 80°; m ∠QRS = __80°__
15. TU = 5, RU = __5__
16. QU + US = 14; QU = __7__
17. Point U is the midpoint of __QS or TR__
18. △QUR ≅ __△SUT__
19. QS = 7, QU = __3.5__
20. ∠3 ≅ __∠2__

▱TQRS

59 — Rectangles, Rhombuses, and Squares

Name _____ Date _____

Rectangle — ▱ with 4 right ∠s — Diagonals are ≅
Rhombus — ▱ with 4 ≅ sides — Diagonals are ⊥
Square — ▱ with 4 right ∠s & 4 ≅ sides — Diagonals are ≅ & ⊥

True or False.

1. A rhombus is a parallelogram with four congruent sides. T
2. A rectangle is a parallelogram with four right angles. T
3. A square is a rectangle and a rhombus. T
4. A rhombus is always a square. F
5. Every parallelogram is a regular quadrilateral. F
6. In a rectangle, the diagonals are perpendicular. F

Rectangle

7. ∠APY, ∠PYT, ∠YTA
8. $\overline{PA}$
9. $\overline{YA}$
10. $\overline{MS}, \overline{BM}, \overline{BD}$
11. $\overline{OD}$
12. 90°

Rhombus

13. $\overline{YM}, \overline{MI}, \overline{TI}$
14. ∠ITV, ∠TVM, ∠VMI
15. $\overline{VI}$

Square

60 — Trapezoids

Exactly one pair of parallel sides.
Exactly two pairs of consecutive angles are supplementary.
∠1 & ∠2,
∠3 & ∠4 are supplementary

base 1
leg   leg
base 2

Parallel sides are bases; non-parallel sides are legs.
Isosceles trapezoids have congruent legs.

1. Name the bases of trapezoid ABCD. $\overline{AB}, \overline{DC}$
2. If m ∠B = 90°, m ∠C = __90°__
3. If m ∠D = 102°, m ∠A = __78°__
4. If EF = 5, GH = __5__
5. If m ∠F = m ∠G & m ∠E = 45°; m ∠G = __135°__
6. m ∠E + __m∠F__ = 180°
7. FG ‖ __EH__
8. If m ∠E = m ∠H and m ∠F = 123°; m ∠E = __57°__ , m ∠G = __123°__
9. If m ∠E = m ∠H and m ∠H = x°; m ∠G = __180−x__ , m ∠F = __180−x__
10. If $\overline{EF} \cong \overline{HG}$, m ∠F __=__ m ∠G

True or False.

11. A trapezoid has two bases. T
12. A trapezoid may have a right angle. T
13. There exists a trapezoid with three congruent sides. T
14. The bases of an isosceles trapezoid are congruent. F
15. The parallel sides of a trapezoid are called the legs. F

Answer Key

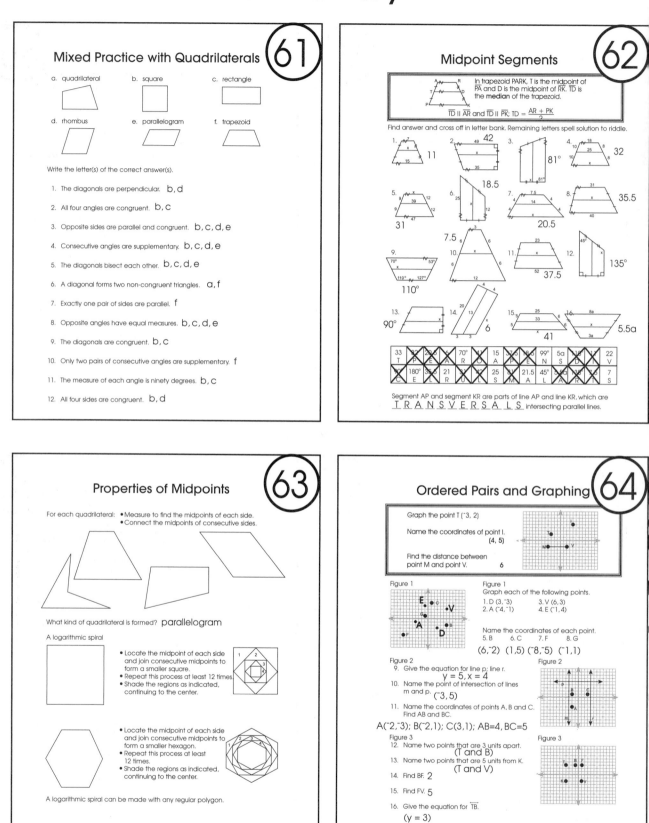

Mixed Practice with Quadrilaterals (61)

a. quadrilateral   b. square   c. rectangle

d. rhombus   e. parallelogram   f. trapezoid

Write the letter(s) of the correct answer(s).

1. The diagonals are perpendicular. b, d
2. All four angles are congruent. b, c
3. Opposite sides are parallel and congruent. b, c, d, e
4. Consecutive angles are supplementary. b, c, d, e
5. The diagonals bisect each other. b, c, d, e
6. A diagonal forms two non-congruent triangles. a, f
7. Exactly one pair of sides are parallel. f
8. Opposite angles have equal measures. b, c, d, e
9. The diagonals are congruent. b, c
10. Only two pairs of consecutive angles are supplementary. f
11. The measure of each angle is ninety degrees. b, c
12. All four sides are congruent. b, d

Midpoint Segments (62)

In trapezoid PARK, T is the midpoint of $\overline{PA}$ and D is the midpoint of $\overline{RK}$. $\overline{TD}$ is the **median** of the trapezoid.

$\overline{TD} \parallel \overline{AR}$ and $\overline{TD} \parallel \overline{PK}$; $TD = \dfrac{AR + PK}{2}$

Find answer and cross off in letter bank. Remaining letters spell solution to riddle.

1. 11
2. 42
3. 81°
4. 32
5. 31
6. 18.5
7. 20.5
8. 35.5
9. 110°
10. 7.5
11. 37.5
12. 135°
13. 90°
14. 6
15. 41
16. 5.5a

33	82	29	70°	15	36	18.5	99°	5a	15	22
T	P	E	A	R	O	A	E	N	S	V
90	180°	35.5	21	6	4	25	6	21.5	45°	35	7
C	E	R	S	M	A	L	A	L	R	S

Segment AP and segment KR are parts of line AP and line KR, which are
T R A N S V E R S A L S intersecting parallel lines.

Properties of Midpoints (63)

For each quadrilateral: • Measure to find the midpoints of each side.
• Connect the midpoints of consecutive sides.

What kind of quadrilateral is formed? parallelogram

A logarithmic spiral

• Locate the midpoint of each side and join consecutive midpoints to form a smaller square.
• Repeat this process at least 12 times.
• Shade the regions as indicated, continuing to the center.

• Locate the midpoint of each side and join consecutive midpoints to form a smaller hexagon.
• Repeat this process at least 12 times.
• Shade the regions as indicated, continuing to the center.

A logarithmic spiral can be made with any regular polygon.

Ordered Pairs and Graphing (64)

Graph the point T (⁻3, 2)

Name the coordinates of point I. (4, 5)

Find the distance between point M and point V. 6

Figure 1
Graph each of the following points.
1. D (3, ⁻3)   3. V (6, 3)
2. A (⁻4, ⁻1)   4. E (⁻1, 4)

Name the coordinates of each point.
5. B   6. C   7. F   8. G
(6, ⁻2) (1, 5) (⁻8, ⁻5) (⁻1, 1)

Figure 2
9. Give the equation for line p; line r.
   y = 5, x = 4
10. Name the point of intersection of lines m and p. (⁻3, 5)
11. Name the coordinates of points A, B and C. Find AB and BC.
   A(⁻2, ⁻3); B(⁻2, 1); C(3, 1); AB=4, BC=5

Figure 3
12. Name two points that are 3 units apart. (T and B)
13. Name two points that are 5 units from K. (T and V)
14. Find BF. 2
15. Find FV. 5
16. Give the equation for $\overleftrightarrow{TB}$. (y = 3)

Answer Key

The Distance Formula ⑥⑤

The distance between 2 points: $(x_1, y_1), (x_2, y_2)$

$D = \sqrt{(x_2 - x_1)^2 + (y_2 - y_1)^2}$

Find the distance between ($^-3$, 2) and (1, $^-2$)

$D = \sqrt{(1 - {}^-3)^2 + ({}^-2 - 2)^2}$
$= \sqrt{(4)^2 + ({}^-4)^2} = \sqrt{16 + 16}$
$= \sqrt{32} = \sqrt{2 \cdot 2 \cdot 2 \cdot 2 \cdot 2}$
$= 4\sqrt{2}$

Find the distance between these pairs of points.

1. (6,4) and (2,1) **5**

2. ($^-2$, $^-4$) and (3,8) **13**

3. (0,0) and (5,10) **$5\sqrt{5}$**

4. ($^-5$,2) and (7,$^-7$) **15**

5. (0,$^-8$) and (8,7) **17**

6. ($^-2$,11) and (4,3) **10**

7. (2,1) and (4,0) **$\sqrt{5}$**

8. (6,4) and (6,$^-2$) **6**

9. ($^-2$,2) and (4,$^-1$) **$3\sqrt{5}$**

10. ($^-3$,$^-5$) and (2,5) **$5\sqrt{5}$**

11. ($^-4$,0) and (2,3) **$3\sqrt{5}$**

12. ($^-1$,5) and (3,$^-3$) **$4\sqrt{5}$**

13. (0,0) and (3,4) **5**

14. (1,8) and (3,10) **$2\sqrt{2}$**

15. (9,8) and ($^-3$,4) **$4\sqrt{10}$**

16. (2,2) and (2,4) **2**

The Midpoint Formula ⑥⑥

To find the coordinates of the midpoint of a segment with endpoints $E_1(x_1, y_1)$ and $E_2(x_2, y_2)$:

$x_m = \dfrac{x_1 + x_2}{2}$ $y_m = \dfrac{y_1 + y_2}{2}$

To find the midpoint of the segment with these endpoints $E_1(^-6, 1)$ and $E_2(3, 7)$:

$x_m = \dfrac{^-6 + 3}{2}$ $y_m = \dfrac{1 + 7}{2}$
$= -\dfrac{3}{2}$ $= 4$

$M\left(-\dfrac{3}{2}, 4\right)$

Find the midpoint of the segments with these endpoints.

1. (1,8) and (3,10) **(2,9)**

2. (2,2) and (2,4) **(2,3)**

3. (2,3) and ($^-1$,$^-5$) **$\left(\dfrac{1}{2},^-1\right)$**

4. (9,8) and ($^-3$,4) **(3,6)**

5. ($^1/_2$,1) and ($4^1/_2$,$^-7$) **$\left(\dfrac{5}{2},^-3\right)$**

6. (0.6,$^-1.2$) and ($^-0.6$,1.2) **(0,0)**

7. ($^-2$,2) and (4,$^-1$) **$\left(1,\dfrac{1}{2}\right)$**

8. ($^-3$,$^-5$) and (2,5) **$\left(-\dfrac{1}{2},0\right)$**

9. ($^-4$,0) and (2,3) **$\left(^-1,\dfrac{3}{2}\right)$**

10. ($^-1$,5) and (3,$^-3$) **(1,1)**

11. (0,0) and (3,4) **$\left(\dfrac{3}{2},2\right)$**

12. (6,4) and (2,1) **$\left(4,\dfrac{5}{2}\right)$**

Given the midpoint and one endpoint of a segment, find the other endpoint.

13. E_1 (5,$^-1$) and M ($^-3$,7) **E_2 ($^-11$,15)**

14. E_1 (2,5) and M ($^-1$,6) **E_2 ($^-4$,7)**

15. E_1 (4,4) and M (3,5) **E_2 (2,6)**

16. E_1 (7,4) and M (3,$^-2$) **E_2 ($^-1$,$^-8$)**

The Slope of a Line ⑥⑦

The slope of a line is the ratio of $\dfrac{\text{rise}}{\text{run}}$.

positive slope   negative slope   slope is 0   slope is undefined

Parallel lines have equal slopes. $m_1 = \dfrac{2}{3}$ $m_2 = \dfrac{2}{3}$

Perpendicular lines have slopes that are negative reciprocals of each other. $m_1 = 4$ $m_2 = -\dfrac{1}{4}$

Note: $4 \cdot -\dfrac{1}{4} = {}^-1$

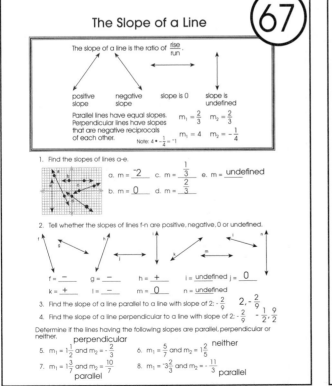

1. Find the slopes of lines a-e.

a. m = **$^-2$**   c. m = **$\dfrac{\frac{1}{3}}{\frac{2}{3}}$**   e. m = **undefined**

b. m = **0**   d. m = **$\dfrac{2}{3}$**

2. Tell whether the slopes of lines f-n are positive, negative, 0 or undefined.

f = **$^-$**   g = **$^-$**   h = **$+$**   i = **undefined**   j = **0**

k = **$+$**   l = **$^-$**   m = **0**   n = **undefined**

3. Find the slope of a line parallel to a line with slope of 2; $-\dfrac{2}{9}$ **2, $-\dfrac{2}{9}$**

4. Find the slope of a line perpendicular to a line with slope of 2; $-\dfrac{2}{9}$ **$-\dfrac{1}{2}, \dfrac{9}{2}$**

Determine if the lines having the following slopes are parallel, perpendicular or neither.

5. $m_1 = 1\dfrac{1}{2}$ and $m_2 = -\dfrac{2}{3}$ **perpendicular**

6. $m_1 = \dfrac{5}{7}$ and $m_2 = 1\dfrac{2}{5}$ **neither**

7. $m_1 = 1\dfrac{3}{7}$ and $m_2 = \dfrac{10}{7}$ **parallel**

8. $m_1 = {}^-3\dfrac{2}{3}$ and $m_2 = -\dfrac{11}{3}$ **parallel**

Polygons with Parallel and Perpendicular ⑥⑧

Parallel lines have slopes that are equal.
Perpendicular lines have slopes that are negative reciprocals of each other.

Determine which sides of quadrilateral QRST are parallel or perpendicular.

Q (0,0)   R (4,2)   S (2,3)   T (0,2)

slope of $\overline{QR} = \dfrac{2-0}{4-0} = \dfrac{1}{2}$ slope of $\overline{ST} = \dfrac{2-3}{0-2} = \dfrac{1}{2}$

slope of $\overline{RS} = \dfrac{3-2}{2-4} = -\dfrac{1}{2}$ slope of $\overline{QT} = \dfrac{2-0}{0-0} =$ undefined

$\overline{QR} \parallel \overline{ST}$

1. Q (0,0)   R (6,$^-2$)   S (7,1)   T (1,3)

$\overline{QR} \perp \overline{RS}$; $\overline{ST} \perp \overline{RS}$; $\overline{QT} \perp \overline{ST}$; $\overline{QT} \perp \overline{RQ}$; $\overline{QR} \parallel \overline{ST}$; $\overline{RS} \parallel \overline{TQ}$

2. Q ($^-3$,$^-1$)   R (3,1)   S (1,3)   T ($^-2$,2)

$\overline{QR} \parallel \overline{ST}$

3. Q (1,$^-3$)   R ($^-2$,0)   S (7,$^-1$)   T (4,2)

$\overline{QS} \parallel \overline{RT}$, $\overline{RQ} \parallel \overline{TS}$

4. Q (2,$^-2$)   R (5,0)   S (1,4)   T ($^-5$,0)

Determine if $\triangle ABC$ is a right triangle. Then, classify it as scalene, isosceles or equilateral. (Hint: Use slope and distance formulas.)

5. A ($^-2$,3)   B (1,5)   C (3,2) **right$\triangle$; isosceles**

6. A (0,0)   B (3,$^-1$)   C (1,2) **not right$\triangle$; scalene**

7. A ($^-3$,0)   B (0,$^-4$)   C (0,0) **right$\triangle$; scalene**

8. A (1,1)   B (1,5)   C (3,3) **not right$\triangle$; isosceles**

Answer Key

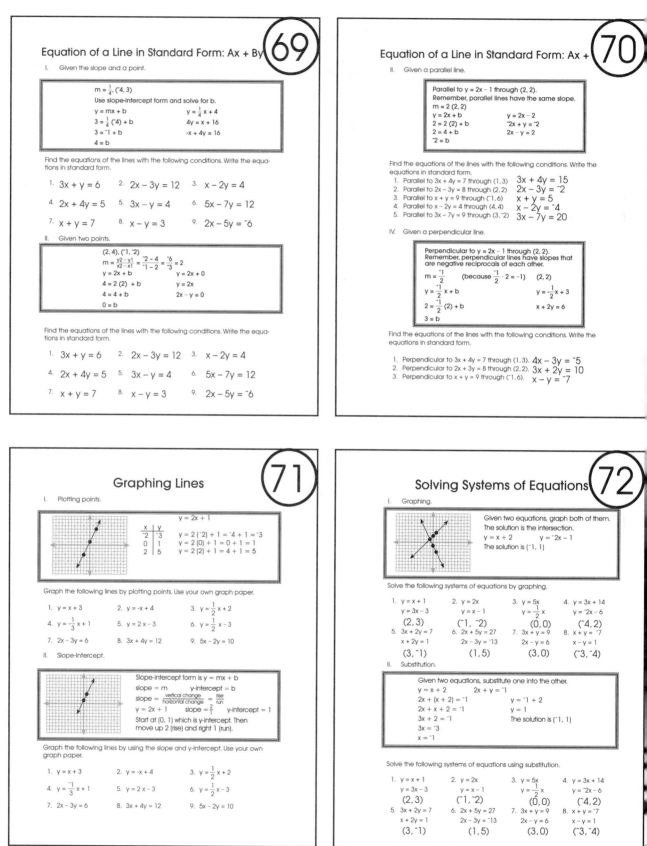

Equation of a Line in Standard Form: Ax + By 69

I. Given the slope and a point.

$m = \frac{1}{4}, (^-4, 3)$

Use slope-intercept form and solve for b.

$y = mx + b$ $y = \frac{1}{4}x + 4$

$3 = \frac{1}{4}(^-4) + b$ $4y = x + 16$

$3 = ^-1 + b$ $^-x + 4y = 16$

$4 = b$

Find the equations of the lines with the following conditions. Write the equations in standard form.

1. $3x + y = 6$ 2. $2x - 3y = 12$ 3. $x - 2y = 4$

4. $2x + 4y = 5$ 5. $3x - y = 4$ 6. $5x - 7y = 12$

7. $x + y = 7$ 8. $x - y = 3$ 9. $2x - 5y = ^-6$

II. Given two points.

$(2, 4), (^-1, ^-2)$

$m = \frac{y_2 - y_1}{x_2 - x_1} = \frac{^-2 - 4}{^-1 - 2} = \frac{^-6}{^-3} = 2$

$y = 2x + b$ $y = 2x + 0$

$4 = 2(2) + b$ $y = 2x$

$4 = 4 + b$ $2x - y = 0$

$0 = b$

Find the equations of the lines with the following conditions. Write the equations in standard form.

1. $3x + y = 6$ 2. $2x - 3y = 12$ 3. $x - 2y = 4$

4. $2x + 4y = 5$ 5. $3x - y = 4$ 6. $5x - 7y = 12$

7. $x + y = 7$ 8. $x - y = 3$ 9. $2x - 5y = ^-6$

Equation of a Line in Standard Form: Ax + 70

II. Given a parallel line.

Parallel to $y = 2x - 1$ through $(2, 2)$.
Remember, parallel lines have the same slope.

$m = 2 (2, 2)$

$y = 2x + b$ $y = 2x - 2$

$2 = 2(2) + b$ $^-2x + y = ^-2$

$2 = 4 + b$ $2x - y = 2$

$^-2 = b$

Find the equations of the lines with the following conditions. Write the equations in standard form.

1. Parallel to $3x + 4y = 7$ through $(1, 3)$ $3x + 4y = 15$
2. Parallel to $2x - 3y = 8$ through $(2, 2)$ $2x - 3y = ^-2$
3. Parallel to $x + y = 9$ through $(^-1, 6)$ $x + y = 5$
4. Parallel to $x - 2y = 4$ through $(4, 4)$ $x - 2y = ^-4$
5. Parallel to $3x - 7y = 9$ through $(3, ^-2)$ $3x - 7y = 20$

IV. Given a perpendicular line.

Perpendicular to $y = 2x - 1$ through $(2, 2)$.
Remember, perpendicular lines have slopes that are negative reciprocals of each other.

$m = \frac{^-1}{2}$ (because $\frac{^-1}{2} \cdot 2 = -1$) $(2, 2)$

$y = \frac{^-1}{2}x + b$ $y = \frac{^-1}{2}x + 3$

$2 = \frac{^-1}{2}(2) + b$ $x + 2y = 6$

$3 = b$

Find the equations of the lines with the following conditions. Write the equations in standard form.

1. Perpendicular to $3x + 4y = 7$ through $(1, 3)$. $4x - 3y = ^-5$
2. Perpendicular to $2x + 3y = 8$ through $(2, 2)$. $3x + 2y = 10$
3. Perpendicular to $x + y = 9$ through $(^-1, 6)$. $x - y = ^-7$

Graphing Lines 71

I. Plotting points.

$y = 2x + 1$

x	y
$^-2$	$^-3$
0	1
2	5

$y = 2(^-2) + 1 = ^-4 + 1 = ^-3$
$y = 2(0) + 1 = 0 + 1 = 1$
$y = 2(2) + 1 = 4 + 1 = 5$

Graph the following lines by plotting points. Use your own graph paper.

1. $y = x + 3$ 2. $y = -x + 4$ 3. $y = \frac{1}{2}x + 2$

4. $y = \frac{1}{3}x + 1$ 5. $y = 2x - 3$ 6. $y = \frac{1}{2}x - 3$

7. $2x - 3y = 6$ 8. $3x + 4y = 12$ 9. $5x - 2y = 10$

II. Slope-Intercept.

Slope-intercept form is $y = mx + b$
slope = m   y-intercept = b
slope = $\frac{\text{vertical change}}{\text{horizontal change}} = \frac{\text{rise}}{\text{run}}$
$y = 2x + 1$ slope = $\frac{2}{1}$ y-intercept = 1
Start at $(0, 1)$ which is y-intercept. Then move up 2 (rise) and right 1 (run).

Graph the following lines by using the slope and y-intercept. Use your own graph paper.

1. $y = x + 3$ 2. $y = -x + 4$ 3. $y = \frac{1}{2}x + 2$

4. $y = \frac{^-1}{3}x + 1$ 5. $y = 2x - 3$ 6. $y = \frac{1}{2}x - 3$

7. $2x - 3y = 6$ 8. $3x + 4y = 12$ 9. $5x - 2y = 10$

Solving Systems of Equations 72

I. Graphing.

Given two equations, graph both of them. The solution is the intersection.
$y = x + 2$ $y = ^-2x - 1$
The solution is $(^-1, 1)$

Solve the following systems of equations by graphing.

1. $y = x + 1$ 2. $y = 2x$ 3. $y = 5x$ 4. $y = 3x + 14$
   $y = 3x - 3$ $y = x - 1$ $y = \frac{1}{2}x$ $y = ^-2x - 6$
   $(2, 3)$ $(^-1, ^-2)$ $(0, 0)$ $(^-4, 2)$

5. $3x + 2y = 7$ 6. $2x + 5y = 27$ 7. $3x + y = 9$ 8. $x + y = ^-7$
   $x + 2y = 1$ $2x - 3y = ^-13$ $2x - y = 6$ $x - y = 1$
   $(3, ^-1)$ $(1, 5)$ $(3, 0)$ $(^-3, ^-4)$

II. Substitution.

Given two equations, substitute one into the other.
$y = x + 2$ $2x + y = ^-1$
$2x + (x + 2) = ^-1$ $y = ^-1 + 2$
$2x + x + 2 = ^-1$ $y = 1$
$3x + 2 = ^-1$ The solution is $(^-1, 1)$
$3x = ^-3$
$x = ^-1$

Solve the following systems of equations using substitution.

1. $y = x + 1$ 2. $y = 2x$ 3. $y = 5x$ 4. $y = 3x + 14$
   $y = 3x - 3$ $y = x - 1$ $y = \frac{1}{2}x$ $y = ^-2x - 6$
   $(2, 3)$ $(^-1, ^-2)$ $(0, 0)$ $(^-4, 2)$

5. $3x + 2y = 7$ 6. $2x + 5y = 27$ 7. $3x + y = 9$ 8. $x + y = ^-7$
   $x + 2y = 1$ $2x - 3y = ^-13$ $2x - y = 6$ $x - y = 1$
   $(3, ^-1)$ $(1, 5)$ $(3, 0)$ $(^-3, ^-4)$

Answer Key

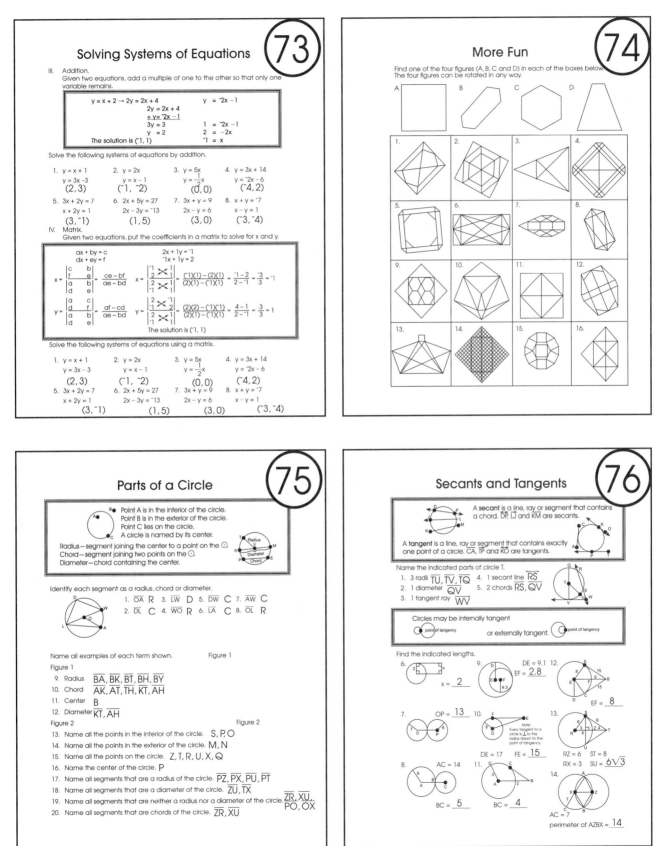

Solving Systems of Equations (73)

III. Addition.
Given two equations, add a multiple of one to the other so that only one variable remains.

$$y = x + 2 \rightarrow 2y = 2x + 4 \qquad y = {}^{-}2x - 1$$
$$2y = 2x + 4$$
$$\underline{+\; y = {}^{-}2x - 1}$$
$$3y = 3 \qquad 1 = {}^{-}2x - 1$$
$$y = 2 \qquad 2 = {}^{-}2x$$
$$\text{The solution is } ({}^{-}1, 1) \qquad {}^{-}1 = x$$

Solve the following systems of equations by addition.

1. $y = x + 1$
$y = 3x - 3$
$(2, 3)$

2. $y = 2x$
$y = x - 1$
$({}^{-}1, {}^{-}2)$

3. $y = 5x$
$y = -\frac{1}{2}x$
$(0, 0)$

4. $y = 3x + 14$
$y = {}^{-}2x - 6$
$({}^{-}4, 2)$

5. $3x + 2y = 7$
$x + 2y = 1$
$(3, {}^{-}1)$

6. $2x + 5y = 27$
$2x - 3y = {}^{-}13$
$(1, 5)$

7. $3x + y = 9$
$2x - y = 6$
$(3, 0)$

8. $x + y = {}^{-}7$
$x - y = 1$
$({}^{-}3, {}^{-}4)$

IV. Matrix.
Given two equations, put the coefficients in a matrix to solve for x and y.

$$ax + by = c \qquad 2x + 1y = {}^{-}1$$
$$dx + ey = f \qquad {}^{-}1x + 1y = 2$$

$$x = \frac{\begin{vmatrix} c & b \\ f & e \end{vmatrix}}{\begin{vmatrix} a & b \\ d & e \end{vmatrix}} = \frac{ce - bf}{ae - bd} \quad x = \frac{\begin{vmatrix} {}^{-}1 & 1 \\ 2 & 1 \end{vmatrix}}{\begin{vmatrix} 2 & 1 \\ {}^{-}1 & 1 \end{vmatrix}} = \frac{({}^{-}1)(1) - (2)(1)}{(2)(1) - ({}^{-}1)(1)} = \frac{{}^{-}1 - 2}{2 - {}^{-}1} = \frac{{}^{-}3}{3} = {}^{-}1$$

$$y = \frac{\begin{vmatrix} a & c \\ d & f \end{vmatrix}}{\begin{vmatrix} a & b \\ d & e \end{vmatrix}} = \frac{af - cd}{ae - bd} \quad y = \frac{\begin{vmatrix} 2 & {}^{-}1 \\ {}^{-}1 & 2 \end{vmatrix}}{\begin{vmatrix} 2 & 1 \\ {}^{-}1 & 1 \end{vmatrix}} = \frac{(2)(2) - ({}^{-}1)({}^{-}1)}{(2)(1) - ({}^{-}1)(1)} = \frac{4 - 1}{2 - {}^{-}1} = \frac{3}{3} = 1$$

The solution is $({}^{-}1, 1)$

Solve the following systems of equations using a matrix.

1. $y = x + 1$
$y = 3x - 3$
$(2, 3)$

2. $y = 2x$
$y = x - 1$
$({}^{-}1, {}^{-}2)$

3. $y = 5x$
$y = -\frac{1}{2}x$
$(0, 0)$

4. $y = 3x + 14$
$y = {}^{-}2x - 6$
$({}^{-}4, 2)$

5. $3x + 2y = 7$
$x + 2y = 1$
$(3, {}^{-}1)$

6. $2x + 5y = 27$
$2x - 3y = {}^{-}13$
$(1, 5)$

7. $3x + y = 9$
$2x - y = 6$
$(3, 0)$

8. $x + y = {}^{-}7$
$x - y = 1$
$({}^{-}3, {}^{-}4)$

More Fun (74)

Find one of the four figures (A, B, C and D) in each of the boxes below. The four figures can be rotated in any way.

A   B   C   D

(boxes 1–16 with figures)

Parts of a Circle (75)

Point A is in the interior of the circle.
Point B is in the exterior of the circle.
Point C lies on the circle.
A circle is named by its center.

Radius—segment joining the center to a point on the ⊙.
Chord—segment joining two points on the ⊙.
Diameter—chord containing the center.

Identify each segment as a radius, chord or diameter.

1. $\overline{OA}$ R
2. $\overline{DL}$ C
3. $\overline{LW}$ D
4. $\overline{WO}$ R
5. $\overline{DW}$ C
6. $\overline{LA}$ C
7. $\overline{AW}$ C
8. $\overline{OL}$ R

Name all examples of each term shown.   Figure 1

Figure 1
9. Radius $\overline{BA}, \overline{BK}, \overline{BT}, \overline{BH}, \overline{BY}$
10. Chord $\overline{AK}, \overline{AT}, \overline{TH}, \overline{KT}, \overline{AH}$
11. Center B
12. Diameter $\overline{KT}, \overline{AH}$

Figure 2   Figure 2
13. Name all the points in the interior of the circle. S, P, O
14. Name all the points in the exterior of the circle. M, N
15. Name all the points on the circle. Z, T, R, U, X, Q
16. Name the center of the circle. P
17. Name all segments that are a radius of the circle. $\overline{PZ}, \overline{PX}, \overline{PU}, \overline{PT}$
18. Name all segments that are a diameter of the circle. $\overline{ZU}, \overline{TX}$
19. Name all segments that are neither a radius nor a diameter of the circle. $\overline{ZR}, \overline{XU}, \overline{PO}, \overline{OX}$
20. Name all segments that are chords of the circle. $\overline{ZR}, \overline{XU}$

Secants and Tangents (76)

A **secant** is a line, ray or segment that contains a chord. $\overleftrightarrow{DP}$, $\overleftrightarrow{LJ}$ and $\overline{KM}$ are secants.

A **tangent** is a line, ray or segment that contains exactly one point of a circle. $\overleftrightarrow{CA}$, $\overrightarrow{TP}$ and $\overrightarrow{KO}$ are tangents.

Name the indicated parts of circle T.
1. 3 radii $\overline{TU}, \overline{TV}, \overline{TQ}$
2. 1 diameter $\overline{QV}$
3. 1 tangent ray $\overrightarrow{WV}$
4. 1 secant line $\overleftrightarrow{RS}$
5. 2 chords $\overline{RS}, \overline{QV}$

Circles may be internally tangent
point of tangency
or externally tangent.
point of tangency

Find the indicated lengths.

6. $x = \underline{2}$
7. $OP = \underline{13}$
8. $AC = 14$ $BC = \underline{5}$
9. $DE = 9.1$ $EF = \underline{2.8}$
10. $DE = 17$ $FE = \underline{15}$
11. $BC = \underline{4}$
12. $EF = \underline{8}$
13. $RZ = 6$ $ST = 8$ $RX = 3$ $SU = \underline{6\sqrt{3}}$
14. $AC = 7$ perimeter of AZBX = $\underline{14}$

Note: Every tangent to a circle is ⊥ to the radius drawn to the point of tangency.

Answer Key

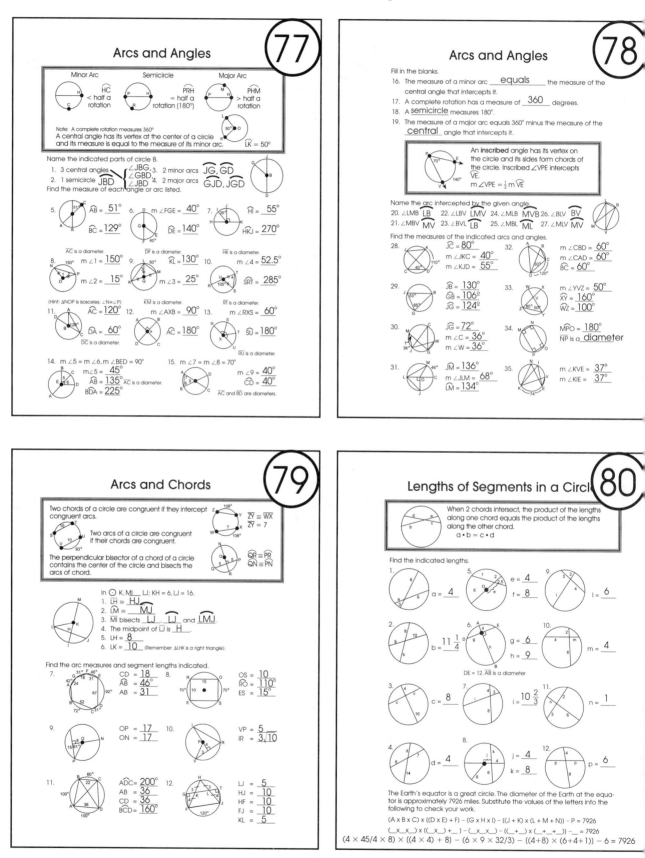

77 — Arcs and Angles

Minor Arc — $\overset{\frown}{HC}$ < half a rotation

Semicircle — $\overset{\frown}{PRH}$ = half a rotation (180°)

Major Arc — $\overset{\frown}{PHM}$ > half a rotation

Note: A complete rotation measures 360°
A central angle has its vertex at the center of a circle and its measure is equal to the measure of its minor arc. $\overset{\frown}{LK} = 50°$

Name the indicated parts of circle B.
1. 3 central angles — $\angle JBG, \angle GBD, \angle JBD$
2. 1 semicircle — $\overset{\frown}{JBD}$
3. 2 minor arcs — $\overset{\frown}{JG}, \overset{\frown}{GD}$
4. 2 major arcs — $\overset{\frown}{GJD}, \overset{\frown}{JGD}$

Find the measure of each angle or arc listed.
5. $\overset{\frown}{AB} = \underline{51°}$, $\overset{\frown}{BC} = \underline{129°}$
6. $m\angle FGE = \underline{40°}$, $\overset{\frown}{DE} = \underline{140°}$
7. $\overset{\frown}{HI} = \underline{55°}$, $\overset{\frown}{HKJ} = \underline{270°}$

$\overline{AC}$ is a diameter.
8. $m\angle 1 = \underline{150°}$, $m\angle 2 = \underline{15°}$
(Hint: △NOP is isosceles: $\angle N = \angle P$)

$\overline{DF}$ is a diameter.
9. $\overset{\frown}{KL} = \underline{130°}$, $m\angle 3 = \underline{25°}$

$\overline{HK}$ is a diameter.
10. $m\angle 4 = \underline{52.5°}$, $\overset{\frown}{SRT} = \underline{285°}$

$\overline{KM}$ is a diameter.
11. $\overset{\frown}{AC} = \underline{120°}$, $\overset{\frown}{DA} = \underline{60°}$
$\overline{DC}$ is a diameter.

12. $m\angle AXB = \underline{90°}$, $\overset{\frown}{AC} = \underline{180°}$

$\overline{RT}$ is a diameter.
13. $m\angle RXS = \underline{60°}$, $\overset{\frown}{SU} = \underline{180°}$
$\overline{RU}$ is a diameter.

14. $m\angle 5 = m\angle 6$, $m\overset{\frown}{BED} = 90°$
$m\angle 5 = \underline{45°}$, $\overset{\frown}{AB} = \underline{135°}$ $\overline{AC}$ is a diameter.
$\overset{\frown}{BDA} = \underline{225°}$

15. $m\angle 7 = m\angle 8 = 70°$
$m\angle 9 = \underline{40°}$, $\overset{\frown}{CD} = \underline{40°}$
$\overline{AC}$ and $\overline{BD}$ are diameters.

78 — Arcs and Angles

Fill in the blanks.
16. The measure of a minor arc __equals__ the measure of the central angle that intercepts it.
17. A complete rotation has a measure of __360__ degrees.
18. A __semicircle__ measures 180°.
19. The measure of a major arc equals 360° minus the measure of the __central__ angle that intercepts it.

An **inscribed** angle has its vertex on the circle and its sides form chords of the circle. Inscribed $\angle VPE$ intercepts $\overset{\frown}{VE}$.
$m\angle VPE = \frac{1}{2}m\overset{\frown}{VE}$

Name the arc intercepted by the given angle.
20. $\angle LMB$ — $\overset{\frown}{LB}$ 22. $\angle LBV$ — $\overset{\frown}{LMV}$ 24. $\angle MLB$ — $\overset{\frown}{MVB}$ 26. $\angle BLV$ — $\overset{\frown}{BV}$
21. $\angle MBV$ — $\overset{\frown}{MV}$ 23. $\angle BVL$ — $\overset{\frown}{LB}$ 25. $\angle MBL$ — $\overset{\frown}{ML}$ 27. $\angle MLV$ — $\overset{\frown}{MV}$

Find the measures of the indicated arcs and angles.
28. $\overset{\frown}{JC} = \underline{80°}$, $m\angle JKC = \underline{40°}$, $m\angle KJD = \underline{55°}$
32. $m\angle CBD = \underline{60°}$, $m\angle CAD = \underline{60°}$, $\overset{\frown}{BC} = \underline{60°}$
29. $\overset{\frown}{JB} = \underline{130°}$, $\overset{\frown}{GB} = \underline{106°}$, $\overset{\frown}{JG} = \underline{124°}$
33. $m\angle YVZ = \underline{50°}$, $\overset{\frown}{XY} = \underline{160°}$, $\overset{\frown}{WZ} = \underline{100°}$
30. $\overset{\frown}{JG} = \underline{72°}$, $m\angle C = \underline{36°}$, $m\angle W = \underline{36°}$
34. $\overset{\frown}{MPO} = \underline{180°}$, $\overline{NP}$ is a __diameter__
31. $\overset{\frown}{JM} = \underline{136°}$, $m\angle JLM = \underline{68°}$, $\overset{\frown}{LM} = \underline{134°}$
35. $m\angle KVE = \underline{37°}$, $m\angle KIE = \underline{37°}$

79 — Arcs and Chords

Two chords of a circle are congruent if they intercept congruent arcs. $\overline{ZY} \cong \overline{WX}$ $\overline{ZY} = 7$

Two arcs of a circle are congruent if their chords are congruent.

The perpendicular bisector of a chord of a circle contains the center of the circle and bisects the arcs of chord. $\overset{\frown}{QR} \cong \overset{\frown}{PR}$ $\overline{QN} \cong \overline{PN}$

In $\odot$ K, $\overset{\frown}{ML} \cong \overset{\frown}{LJ}$; KH = 6, LJ = 16.
1. $\overline{LH} \cong \underline{\overline{HJ}}$
2. $\overset{\frown}{LM} = \underline{\overset{\frown}{MJ}}$
3. $\overset{\frown}{MI}$ bisects $\underline{\overset{\frown}{LJ}}$, $\underline{\overset{\frown}{LJ}}$ and $\underline{\overset{\frown}{LMJ}}$.
4. The midpoint of $\overline{LJ}$ is $\underline{H}$.
5. LH = $\underline{8}$
6. LK = $\underline{10}$ (Remember: △LHK is a right triangle).

Find the arc measures and segment lengths indicated.
7. $\overset{\frown}{CD} = \underline{18}$, $\overset{\frown}{AB} = \underline{46°}$, AB = $\underline{31}$
8. OS = $\underline{10}$, $\overset{\frown}{RO} = \underline{110°}$, ES = $\underline{15}$
9. OP = $\underline{17}$, ON = $\underline{17}$
10. VP = $\underline{5}$, IR = $\underline{3\sqrt{10}}$
11. $\overset{\frown}{ADC} = \underline{200°}$, AB = $\underline{36}$, CD = $\underline{36}$, $\overset{\frown}{BCD} = \underline{160°}$
12. LJ = $\underline{5}$, HJ = $\underline{10}$, HF = $\underline{10}$, FJ = $\underline{10}$, KL = $\underline{5}$

80 — Lengths of Segments in a Circle

When 2 chords intersect, the product of the lengths along one chord equals the product of the lengths along the other chord.
$a \cdot b = c \cdot d$

Find the indicated lengths.
1. $a = \underline{4}$
5. $e = \underline{4}$, $f = \underline{8}$
9. $I = \underline{6}$
2. $b = \underline{11\frac{1}{4}}$
6. $g = \underline{6}$, $h = \underline{9}$ DE = 12. $\overline{AB}$ is a diameter
10. $m = \underline{4}$
3. $c = \underline{8}$
7. $i = \underline{10\frac{2}{3}}$
11. $n = \underline{1}$
4. $d = \underline{4}$
8. $j = \underline{4}$, $k = \underline{8}$
12. $p = \underline{6}$

The Earth's equator is a great circle. The diameter of the Earth at the equator is approximately 7926 miles. Substitute the values of the letters into the following to check your work.
$(A \times B \times C) \times ((D \times E) + F) - (G \times H \times I) - ((J + K) \times (L + M + N)) - P = 7926$
$(\_\times\_\times\_) \times ((\_\times\_) + \_) - (\_\times\_\times\_) - ((\_+\_) \times (\_+\_+\_)) - \_ = 7926$
$(4 \times 45/4 \times 8) \times ((4 \times 4) + 8) - (6 \times 9 \times 32/3) - ((4+8) \times (6+4+1)) - 6 = 7926$

Answer Key

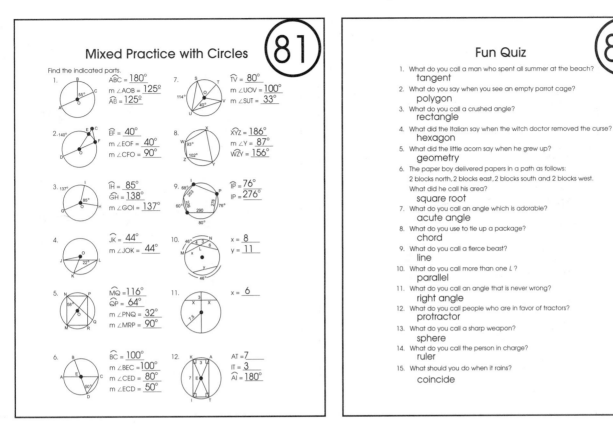

Mixed Practice with Circles (81)

Find the indicated parts.

1. $\overset{\frown}{ABC} = \underline{180°}$
m $\angle AOB = \underline{125°}$
$\overset{\frown}{AB} = \underline{125°}$

2. $\overset{\frown}{EF} = \underline{40°}$
m $\angle EOF = \underline{40°}$
m $\angle CFO = \underline{90°}$

3. $\overset{\frown}{IH} = \underline{85°}$
$\overset{\frown}{GH} = \underline{138°}$
m $\angle GOI = \underline{137°}$

4. $\overset{\frown}{JK} = \underline{44°}$
m $\angle JOK = \underline{44°}$

5. $\overset{\frown}{MQ} = \underline{116°}$
$\overset{\frown}{QP} = \underline{64°}$
m $\angle PNQ = \underline{32°}$
m $\angle MRP = \underline{90°}$

6. $\overset{\frown}{BC} = \underline{100°}$
m $\angle BEC = \underline{100°}$
m $\angle CED = \underline{80°}$
m $\angle ECD = \underline{50°}$

7. $\overset{\frown}{TV} = \underline{80°}$
m $\angle UOV = \underline{100°}$
m $\angle SUT = \underline{33°}$

8. $\overset{\frown}{XYZ} = \underline{186°}$
m $\angle Y = \underline{87°}$
$\overset{\frown}{WZY} = \underline{156°}$

9. $\overset{\frown}{IP} = \underline{76°}$
$IP = \underline{276°}$

10. $x = \underline{8}$
$y = \underline{11}$

11. $x = \underline{6}$

12. $AT = \underline{7}$
$IT = \underline{3}$
$\overset{\frown}{AI} = \underline{180°}$

Fun Quiz (82)

1. What do you call a man who spent all summer at the beach?
tangent
2. What do you say when you see an empty parrot cage?
polygon
3. What do you call a crushed angle?
rectangle
4. What did the Italian say when the witch doctor removed the curse?
hexagon
5. What did the little acorn say when he grew up?
geometry
6. The paper boy delivered papers in a path as follows:
2 blocks north, 2 blocks east, 2 blocks south and 2 blocks west.
What did he call his area?
square root
7. What do you call an angle which is adorable?
acute angle
8. What do you use to tie up a package?
chord
9. What do you call a fierce beast?
line
10. What do you call more than one *L*?
parallel
11. What do you call an angle that is never wrong?
right angle
12. What do you call people who are in favor of tractors?
protractor
13. What do you call a sharp weapon?
sphere
14. What do you call the person in charge?
ruler
15. What should you do when it rains?
coincide

Perimeter (83)

The perimeter of a figure is the distance around the outside.
$P = 4 + 4 + 5 + 5$
$P = 18$

Find the perimeter.

1. 20
2. 16
3. 24
4. 12
5. 17
6. 10
7. 25
8. 23
9. 38
10. 56
11. 50
12. 64

Perimeters and Ratios (84)

In similar figures, the ratio of the perimeter is equal to the ratio of any pair of sides.
$\frac{1}{2} =$ sides $\frac{4}{8} = \frac{1}{2}$ perimeter

Find the missing perimeter, ratio or labeled side. (All figures are similar.)

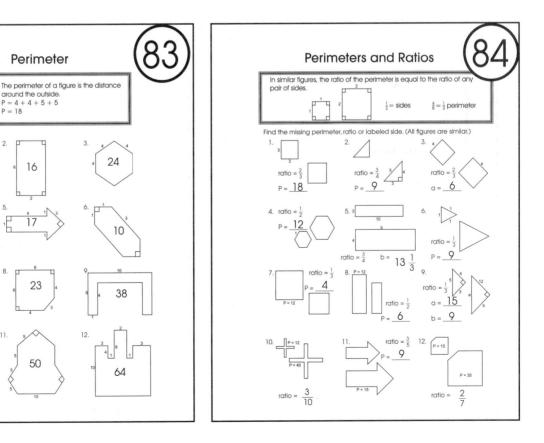

1. ratio $= \frac{2}{3}$
P = 18
2. ratio $= \frac{3}{4}$
P = 9
3. ratio $= \frac{2}{3}$
a = 6
4. ratio $= \frac{1}{2}$
P = 12
5. ratio $= \frac{3}{4}$ b = $13\frac{1}{3}$
6. ratio $= \frac{1}{3}$
P = 9
7. ratio $= \frac{1}{3}$ P = 4
8. P = 12   ratio $= \frac{1}{2}$ P = 6
9. ratio $= \frac{1}{3}$ a = 15   b = 9
10. ratio $= \frac{3}{10}$
11. ratio $= \frac{3}{5}$ P = 9
12. ratio $= \frac{2}{7}$

Answer Key

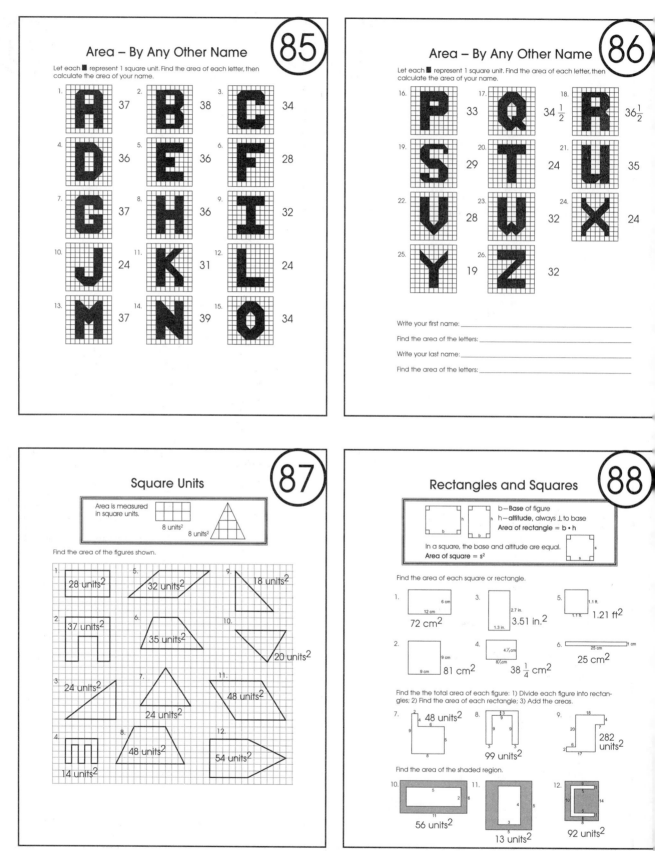

Area – By Any Other Name (85)

Let each ■ represent 1 square unit. Find the area of each letter, then calculate the area of your name.

1. A 37
2. B 38
3. C 34
4. D 36
5. E 36
6. F 28
7. G 37
8. H 36
9. I 32
10. J 24
11. K 31
12. L 24
13. M 37
14. N 39
15. O 34

Area – By Any Other Name (86)

Let each ■ represent 1 square unit. Find the area of each letter, then calculate the area of your name.

16. P 33
17. Q $34\frac{1}{2}$
18. R $36\frac{1}{2}$
19. S 29
20. T 24
21. U 35
22. V 28
23. W 32
24. X 24
25. Y 19
26. Z 32

Write your first name: _____

Find the area of the letters: _____

Write your last name: _____

Find the area of the letters: _____

Square Units (87)

Area is measured in square units.
8 units²   8 units²

Find the area of the figures shown.

1. 28 units²
5. 32 units²
9. 18 units²
2. 37 units²
6. 35 units²
10. 20 units²
3. 24 units²
7. 24 units²
11. 48 units²
4. 14 units²
8. 48 units²
12. 54 units²

Rectangles and Squares (88)

b—Base of figure
h—altitude, always ⊥ to base
Area of rectangle = b • h

In a square, the base and altitude are equal.
Area of square = s²

Find the area of each square or rectangle.

1. 12 cm, 6 cm → 72 cm²
3. 2.7 in., 1.3 in. → 3.51 in.²
5. 1.1 ft, 1.1 ft → 1.21 ft²
2. 9 cm, 9 cm → 81 cm²
4. $4\frac{1}{2}$ cm, $8\frac{1}{2}$ cm → $38\frac{1}{4}$ cm²
6. 25 cm, 1 cm → 25 cm²

Find the the total area of each figure: 1) Divide each figure into rectangles; 2) Find the area of each rectangle; 3) Add the areas.

7. 48 units²
8. 99 units²
9. 282 units²

Find the area of the shaded region.

10. 56 units²
11. 13 units²
12. 92 units²

Answer Key

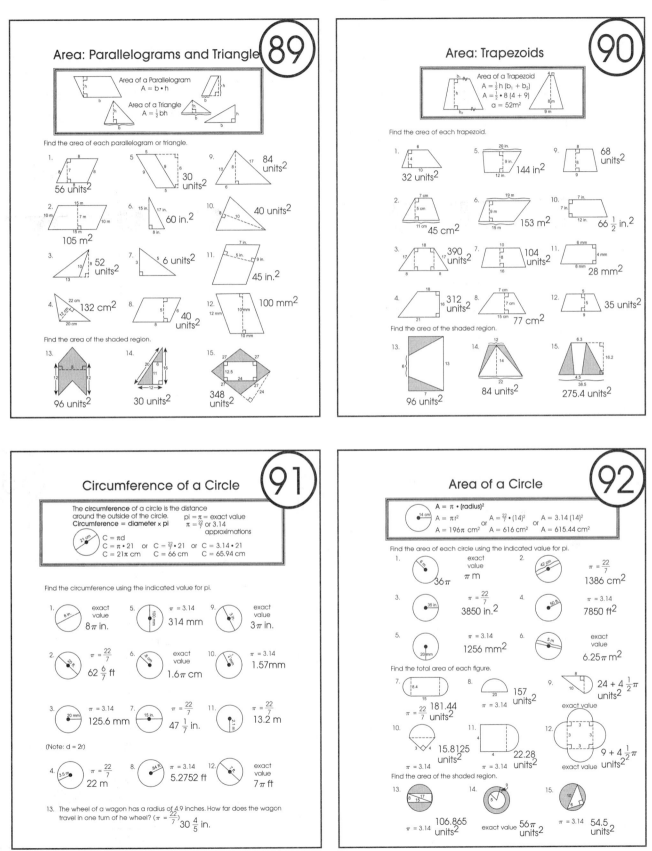

(89) Area: Parallelograms and Triangles

Area of a Parallelogram
$A = b \cdot h$

Area of a Triangle
$A = \frac{1}{2} bh$

Find the area of each parallelogram or triangle.

1. 56 units²
2. 105 m²
3. 52 units²
4. 132 cm²
5. 30 units²
6. 60 in.²
7. 6 units²
8. 40 units²
9. 84 units²
10. 40 units²
11. 45 in.²
12. 100 mm²

Find the area of the shaded region.

13. 96 units²
14. 30 units²
15. 348 units²

(90) Area: Trapezoids

Area of a Trapezoid
$A = \frac{1}{2} h (b_1 + b_2)$
$A = \frac{1}{2} \cdot 8 (4 + 9)$
$a = 52 m^2$

Find the area of each trapezoid.

1. 32 units²
2. 45 cm²
3. 390 units²
4. 312 units²
5. 144 in²
6. 153 m²
7. 104 units²
8. 77 cm²
9. 68 units²
10. 66 ½ in.²
11. 28 mm²
12. 35 units²

Find the area of the shaded region.

13. 96 units²
14. 84 units²
15. 275.4 units²

(91) Circumference of a Circle

The **circumference** of a circle is the distance around the outside of the circle.
Circumference = diameter x pi
pi = π = exact value
$\pi = \frac{22}{7}$ or 3.14 approximations

$C = \pi d$
$C = \pi \cdot 21$ or $C = \frac{22}{7} \cdot 21$ or $C = 3.14 \cdot 21$
$C = 21\pi$ cm $C = 66$ cm $C = 65.94$ cm

Find the circumference using the indicated value for pi.

1. exact value — 8π in.
2. $\pi = \frac{22}{7}$ — 62 6/7 ft
3. π = 3.14 — 125.6 mm
4. $\pi = \frac{22}{7}$ — 22 m
5. π = 3.14 — 314 mm
6. exact value — 1.6π cm
7. $\pi = \frac{22}{7}$ — 47 1/7 in.
8. π = 3.14 — 5.2752 ft
9. exact value — 3π in.
10. π = 3.14 — 1.57 mm
11. $\pi = \frac{22}{7}$ — 13.2 m
12. exact value — 7π ft

(Note: d = 2r)

13. The wheel of a wagon has a radius of 4.9 inches. How far does the wagon travel in one turn of the wheel? $(\pi = \frac{22}{7})$ 30 4/5 in.

(92) Area of a Circle

$A = \pi \cdot (radius)^2$
$A = \pi r^2$ or $A = \frac{22}{7} \cdot (14)^2$ or $A = 3.14 (14)^2$
$A = 196\pi$ cm² $A = 616$ cm² $A = 615.44$ cm²

Find the area of each circle using the indicated value for pi.

1. exact value — 36π m
2. $\pi = \frac{22}{7}$ — 1386 cm²
3. $\pi = \frac{22}{7}$ — 3850 in.²
4. π = 3.14 — 7850 ft²
5. π = 3.14 — 1256 mm²
6. exact value — 6.25π m²

Find the total area of each figure.

7. $\pi = \frac{22}{7}$ — 181.44 units²
8. π = 3.14 — 157 units²
9. exact value — 24 + 4 ½ π units²
10. π = 3.14 — 15.8125 units²
11. π = 3.14 — 22.28 units²
12. exact value — 9 + 4 ½ π units²

Find the area of the shaded region.

13. π = 3.14 — 106.865 units²
14. exact value — 56π units²
15. π = 3.14 — 54.5 units²

Answer Key

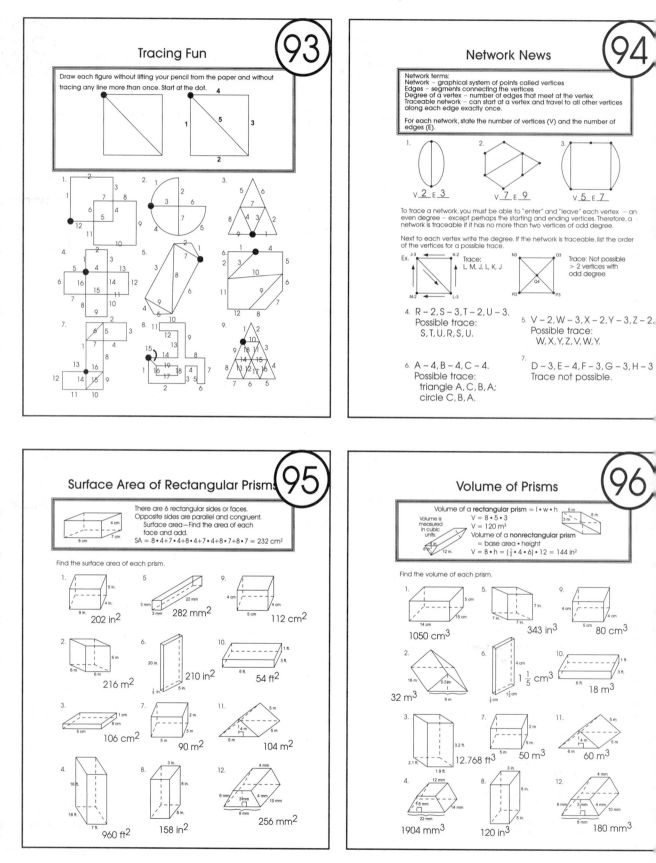

Answer Key

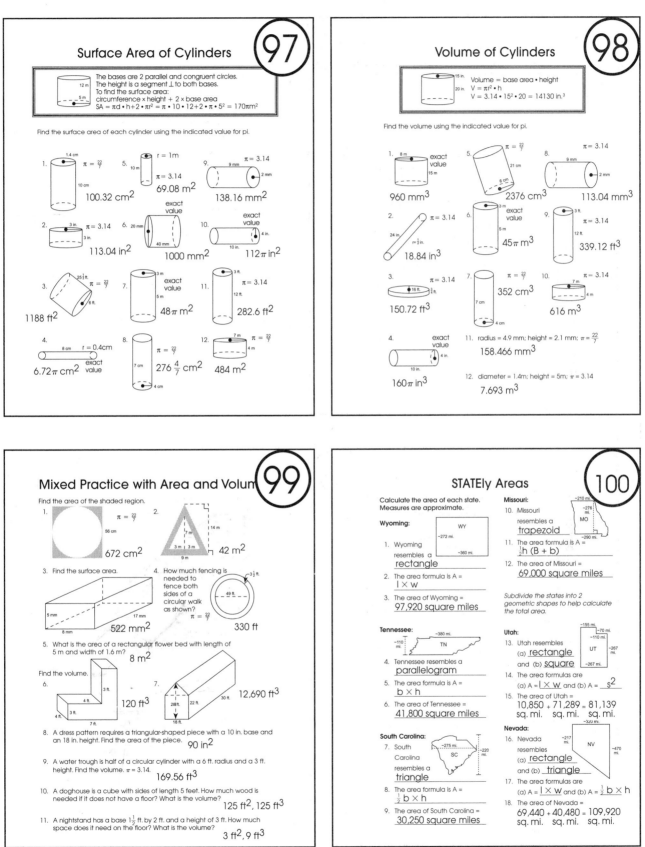

97 Surface Area of Cylinders

The bases are 2 parallel and congruent circles.
The height is a segment ⊥ to both bases.
To find the surface area:
circumference × height + 2 × base area
$SA = \pi d \cdot h + 2 \cdot \pi r^2 = \pi \cdot 10 \cdot 12 + 2 \cdot \pi \cdot 5^2 = 170\pi m^2$

Find the surface area of each cylinder using the indicated value for pi.

1. $\pi = \frac{22}{7}$ 100.32 cm^2
2. $\pi = 3.14$ 113.04 in^2
3. $\pi = \frac{22}{7}$ 1188 ft^2
4. r = 0.4cm   exact value $6.72\pi \text{ cm}^2$
5. $\pi = 3.14$ 69.08 m^2
6. exact value 1000 mm^2
7. exact value $48\pi \text{ m}^2$
8. $\pi = \frac{22}{7}$ $276 \frac{4}{7} \text{ cm}^2$
9. $\pi = 3.14$ 138.16 mm^2
10. exact value $112\pi \text{ in}^2$
11. $\pi = 3.14$ 282.6 ft^2
12. $\pi = \frac{22}{7}$ 484 m^2

98 Volume of Cylinders

Volume = base area • height
$V = \pi r^2 \cdot h$
$V = 3.14 \cdot 15^2 \cdot 20 = 14130 \text{ in.}^3$

Find the volume using the indicated value for pi.

1. exact value 960 mm^3
2. $\pi = 3.14$ 18.84 in^3
3. $\pi = 3.14$ 150.72 ft^3
4. exact value $160\pi \text{ in}^3$
5. $\pi = \frac{22}{7}$ 2376 cm^3
6. exact value $45\pi \text{ m}^3$
7. $\pi = \frac{22}{7}$ 352 cm^3
8. $\pi = 3.14$ 113.04 mm^3
9. $\pi = 3.14$ 339.12 ft^3
10. $\pi = 3.14$ 616 m^3
11. radius = 4.9 mm; height = 2.1 mm; $\pi = \frac{22}{7}$ 158.466 mm^3
12. diameter = 1.4m; height = 5m; $\pi = 3.14$ 7.693 m^3

99 Mixed Practice with Area and Volume

Find the area of the shaded region.
1. $\pi = \frac{22}{7}$ 672 cm^2
2. 42 m^2
3. Find the surface area. 522 mm^2
4. How much fencing is needed to fence both sides of a circular walk as shown? $\pi = \frac{22}{7}$ 330 ft
5. What is the area of a rectangular flower bed with length of 5 m and width of 1.6 m? 8 m^2

Find the volume.
6. 120 ft^3
7. $12,690 \text{ ft}^3$
8. A dress pattern requires a triangular-shaped piece with a 10 in. base and an 18 in. height. Find the area of the piece. 90 in^2
9. A water trough is half of a circular cylinder with a 6 ft. radius and a 3 ft. height. Find the volume. $\pi = 3.14$. 169.56 ft^3
10. A doghouse is a cube with sides of length 5 feet. How much wood is needed if it does not have a floor? What is the volume? $125 \text{ ft}^2, 125 \text{ ft}^3$
11. A nightstand has a base $1\frac{1}{2}$ ft. by 2 ft. and a height of 3 ft. How much space does it need on the floor? What is the volume? $3 \text{ ft}^2, 9 \text{ ft}^3$

100 STATEly Areas

Calculate the area of each state. Measures are approximate.

Wyoming:
1. Wyoming resembles a __rectangle__
2. The area formula is A = __l × w__
3. The area of Wyoming = __97,920 square miles__

Tennessee:
4. Tennessee resembles a __parallelogram__
5. The area formula is A = __b × h__
6. The area of Tennessee = __41,800 square miles__

South Carolina:
7. South Carolina resembles a __triangle__
8. The area formula is A = __$\frac{1}{2}$ b × h__
9. The area of South Carolina = __30,250 square miles__

Missouri:
10. Missouri resembles a __trapezoid__
11. The area formula is A = __$\frac{1}{2}$h (B + b)__
12. The area of Missouri = __69,000 square miles__

Subdivide the states into 2 geometric shapes to help calculate the total area.

Utah:
13. Utah resembles (a) __rectangle__ and (b) __square__
14. The area formulas are (a) A = __l × w__ and (b) A = __s^2__
15. The area of Utah = __10,850 + 71,289 = 81,139__ sq. mi. sq. mi. sq. mi.

Nevada:
16. Nevada resembles (a) __rectangle__ and (b) __triangle__
17. The area formulas are (a) A = __l × w__ and (b) A = __$\frac{1}{2}$ b × h__
18. The area of Nevada = __69,440 + 40,480 = 109,920__ sq. mi. sq. mi. sq. mi.

Answer Key

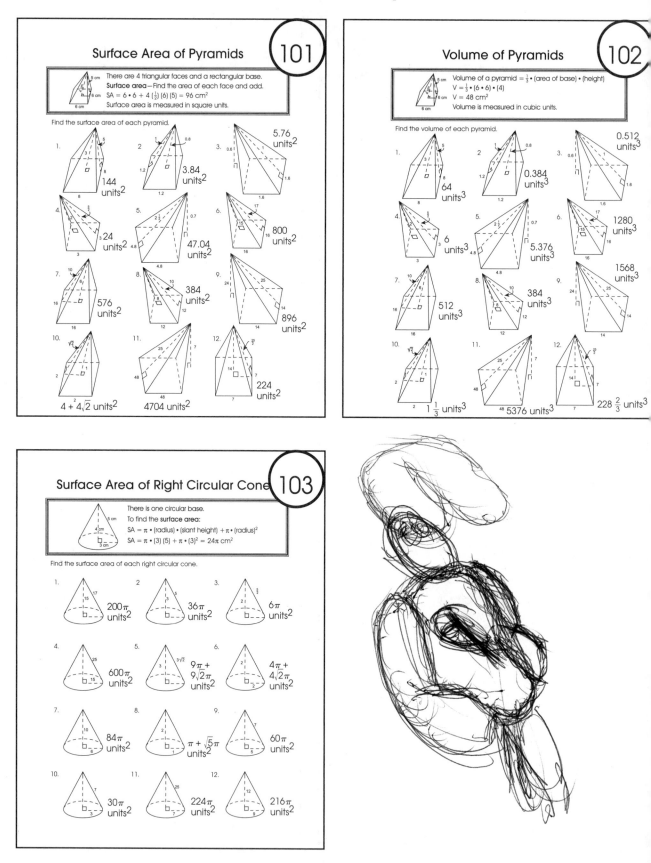

Surface Area of Pyramids (101)

There are 4 triangular faces and a rectangular base.
Surface area—Find the area of each face and add.
SA = 6 • 6 + 4 $(\frac{1}{2})$ (6) (5) = 96 cm²
Surface area is measured in square units.

Find the surface area of each pyramid.

1. 144 units²
2. 3.84 units²
3. 5.76 units²
4. 24 units²
5. 47.04 units²
6. 800 units²
7. 576 units²
8. 384 units²
9. 896 units²
10. $4 + 4\sqrt{2}$ units²
11. 4704 units²
12. 224 units²

Volume of Pyramids (102)

Volume of a pyramid = $\frac{1}{3}$ • (area of base) • (height)
V = $\frac{1}{3}$ • (6 • 6) • (4)
V = 48 cm²
Volume is measured in cubic units.

Find the volume of each pyramid.

1. 64 units³
2. 0.384 units³
3. 0.512 units³
4. 6 units³
5. 5.376 units³
6. 1280 units³
7. 512 units³
8. 384 units³
9. 1568 units³
10. $1\frac{1}{3}$ units³
11. 5376 units³
12. $228\frac{2}{3}$ units³

Surface Area of Right Circular Cone (103)

There is one circular base.
To find the **surface area**:
SA = π • (radius) • (slant height) + π • (radius)²
SA = π • (3) (5) + π • (3)² = 24π cm²

Find the surface area of each right circular cone.

1. 200π units²
2. 36π units²
3. 6π units²
4. 600π units²
5. $9π + 9\sqrt{2}π$ units²
6. $4π + 4\sqrt{2}π$ units²
7. 84π units²
8. $π + \sqrt{5}π$ units²
9. 60π units²
10. 30π units²
11. 224π units²
12. 216π units²